PLAY BETTER GOLF

Great players and what we can learn from them

Watching great players from the past, and the present is part of the tradition of golf. We can marvel at their feats, watch admiringly as they make the game look simple, and we can learn from them. Perhaps we can take a little of the ingredients that made Tiger, Jack, or Babe great and build it into our own game. We may never become world beaters… but we can move forward.

Bobby Jones

Robert Tyre Jones was born on St. Patrick's Day, 1902 in Atlanta, Georgia. He achieved 23 tournament wins in his career, including four wins in The US Open, three in The British Open, five in The US Amateur, and one in The British Amateur.

His success was not achieved easily. Bobby Jones started life as a very sick child whose parents always worried that their frail son might pick up an infection from other children. He was allowed to play golf however and, under the protective eyes of his parents took up the game at about five, using cut-down clubs.

When he was 12, with the help of Scottish golf professional Jimmy Maiden, and through sheer perseverance, Bobby started to shoot rounds in the 70s. By age 14 he had won the Georgia State Open followed by the Southern Amateur Championship. Fans who knew of the young man's exploits expected great results and placed extreme pressure on him to win a Major.

It took a while but, when that win came in the 1923 US Open, there was no stopping him. He dominated for seven years until, suddenly in 1930, he retired from competitive golf. In his last year he completed the Grand Slam of all four Majors, a still unequalled record.

Retirement gave Bobby a few business opportunities and allowed him to retain an interest in golf. These opportunities included the birth of Augusta National and The Masters.

Bobby Jones in action during the 1927 British Open Championship at St Andrews, which he went on to win.

▶ **fact**file

- BORN **17th March 1902**
- DIED **18th December 1971**

Major wins:

- 4 X WINNER **The US Open 1923, 1926, 1929, 1930**
- 3 X WINNER **The British Open 1926, 1927, 1930**
- 5 X WINNER **The US Amateur 1924, 1925, 1927, 1928, 1930**
- 1 X WINNER **The British Amateur 1930**

What you can learn

After playing competitive golf Bobby actually turned professional which allowed him to write instructional books. These books have developed the modern swing, which the world's greatest are trying to emulate.

Bobby Jones had a continuous swing which was smooth and repeatable. With good timing and grace he was able to attack the ball with relaxed hands to gain the best possible results. There is a lot that you can learn from such a legend of the game.

Once good timing has been mastered you will be able to repeat the same movement; this takes the pressure of self-correction away, allowing you to relax in the swing, gaining the best attack position. Although Bobby Jones found it hard to ignore the outside pressures of life he was able to take away any tension from his own swing.

It's good to use something lighter than a golf club to practise a fast rhythmic swing. Here the model uses a specially built tool for increasing rotation and speed. The lighter the tool, the easier it is to build a rhythmic swing.

Remember to focus on the following aspects of your swing:

1 Takeaway—a neutral takeaway is the ideal motion for the start of your swing (see page 87).

2 Check your swing plane as this will ensure consistent striking (see page 89)

3 Impact and club-head speed is vital to generate power and accurate hitting (see page 91)

4 Club-head speed does not just come from the hands but the shoulders, hips and knees. They all generate more speed from each other (see page 90)

5 Correct weight transfer will result in a well balanced "classic" follow through position (see page 86)

Sam Snead

Snead was born into a farming family in Hot Springs, Virginia. He was first introduced to golf when he worked as a caddie at his local hotel. At this time the young Snead had his heart set on football stardom but, having sustained a back injury, Snead's path changed to a lifetime of playing golf.

Snead went on to enjoy a golfing career which stretched over more than 50 years, winning a record 81 PGA titles. Alas, Snead never grasped the title he most wanted; US Open Champion, despite having come second a heart-stopping four times. Snead was famed for the sweetest of swings and his charismatic personality; he became a crowd favorite and was considered a national hero.

Snead played at a time when woods were made of lumber. He was famed for his lengthy drives which would regularly reach 275 yards. His natural swing was the envy of many and a source of inspiration to aspiring big hitters. Despite Snead's "big hits," his approach to the game was remarkably relaxed. He saw the advantage of staying "loose"

and clearing his mind. His was a natural talent. His timing on the fairway was invariably spot-on, although his putting game was not great. He found getting the ball on the green easier

Circa 1955, American golfer Sam 'Slammin' Sammy' Snead demonstrates his famous fluid swing.

> **fact**file

- BORN **27th May 1912**
- DIED **23rd May 2002**

Major wins:

- 3 X WINNER **The Masters 1949, 1952, 1954**
- 1 X WINNER **The British Open 1946**
- 3 X WINNER **US PGA 1942, 1949, 1951**
- 6 X WINNER **PGA Seniors 1964, 1965, 1967, 1970, 1972, 1973**

than playing the green. He tried to correct his putting difficulties by putting from between his legs but such an approach was ruled illegal by the golf authorities. Snead re-emerged with a modified approach; facing the hole with his feet together and putting from the side to great effect.

Snead dominated The Masters, winning in 1949, 1952 and again in 1954 after beating Ben Hogan by only one stroke in an 18-hole play-off. As a (then) record three-time Masters champion, Snead was given the status of honorary starter, continuing to take the first ceremonial swing from 1983 to his final year in 2002, the year of his death.

Snead retired from professional golf in 1974 but at the age of 67 became the first player to ever shoot below his age, making 66 at the Quad Cities Open in 1979. Snead retired as one of the only players to have won tournaments in six decades.

What you can learn

Sam was renowned for his natural flexibility, balanced with strength and stability. This may have come from his farming and football; it was certainly to help him have a long career.

These attributes allowed him to play a more natural game of golf, rather than worrying about set positions in the swing. There are many golfers who repeat one movement which, over time, works and develops the muscles. If this is one-sided it is easy to over-develop muscles which can leave the body imbalanced. The key: try to exercise your body in a balanced manner for longevity in sport.

Figure 1   **Figure 2**   **Figure 3**

In golf it is possible to become one-sided. The exercise above shows how to ensure you are loading both sides of your body equally.

*Starting with **Figure 1**, hold a weighted ball above your head in a neutral position. Figures 2 and 3 show the stretch both to the left (**Figure 2**) and the right (**Figure 3**) in equal distance.*

Ben Hogan

One of three children, Texan Ben Hogan faced early hardship following the suicide of his father, Chester. The family, now living in Forth Worth, all pulled together to raise extra money and Ben grew up selling newspapers. He eventually secured a job as a caddy at the Glen Cargen Country Club which he found to be more to his liking. This is where he met the equally young golfing great, Byron Nelson. Both got very involved with golf and often competed against each other at the club.

Ben turned professional at 17 but this was not an immediate financial success. He combined his playing career with teaching (and many other jobs) but it was a decade before Ben achieved his first tournament win.

Maybe it was confidence, or just a late blossoming of talent but this first win was followed by two more consecutive wins. No one could have predicted what was to follow in the coming years. Described by the likes of Jack Nicklaus as the best-ever ball striker, Ben Hogan achieved 63 professional tournament wins up to 1959 even though his career was interrupted by a near-fatal car accident in 1949.

Ben won his first Major in 1946 and, after a long gap created by World War II, went on to win eight more. In 1953 he achieved what is now known as the Hogan Slam (The Masters, The US Open and The British Open). The only year he was unable to bring a Major home was 1949 following his car accident. Tiger Woods is the only man to have repeated the Hogan slam since 1953.

▷**fact**file
- BORN **13th August 1912**
- DIED **25th July 1997**

Major wins:
- 2 X WINNER **The Masters 1951, 1953**
- 4 X WINNER **The US Open 1948, 1950, 1951, 1953**
- 1 X WINNER **The British Open 1953**
- 2 X WINNER **US PGA 1946, 1948**

Ben Hogan warms up for his Canada Cup match, 1956.

What you can learn

Hogan has been described as one of the greatest ball strikers of all time. You can only be a good striker of the ball if all your moving parts work together. What should always be addressed is how active your body is during your swing. The greatest moving part in the swing is the club head (i.e. it has the longest journey from start to finish), then the arms, shoulders, hips followed by knees and feet. Working from the ground up there should never be more movement from your lower body than the upper body.

There is no point having a 50-degree hip turn when you lack the flexibility to turn your shoulders more than 70 degrees. The ideal ratio would be:

shoulders 70 degrees = hips 35 degrees

If you can increase your shoulder turn to 90 degrees then your hips would be 45 degrees. The key is to swing in the right ratio but within your own physical capabilities.

Figure 1

Figure 2

60°

30°

Your turn will depend on the shot you are making. In this case shoulders at 60 degrees and hips 30 degrees.

90°

45°

A greater turn for a fuller swing but the ratio remains the same

Two examples of the shoulder/hip ratio. The degree of turn depends on your own personal suppleness. A good ratio will be achieved if you don't overstretch.

Babe Zaharias

Mildred Didrikson Zaharias was the greatest female athlete of the first half of the twentieth century. Her nickname Babe came from her love for renowned Baseball player, "Babe" Ruth. She gained her surname of Zaharias when she married the famous wrestler, George Zaharias.

Born in 1914, in Port Arthur, Texas, Babe Zaharias started sporting life as a fine basketball player, earning national honours. She then competed in the National Track & Field Championships, winning six of the eight events she entered... a success that led to her appearance in the 1932 Los Angeles Olympics. She was only permitted to partake in three disciplines at the Games: javelin, 80m hurdles and high jump. She won gold in two of the events (javelin and the 80m hurdles) but was disqualified for an unladylike technique in the high jump!

Then she learned to play golf. She quickly became an outstanding striker of the ball and, with the assistance of English golfer Joyce Wethered, developed the rest of her game. Her all-round game allowed her to go on to win a string of consecutive tournaments, as an amateur, during 1946 and 1947. Babe also picked up The British Ladies Open which had never been won by an American.

Turning professional in 1948 Babe went on to win The US Women's Open three times, the last time in 1954 some 18 months after having surgery for cancer. She also won another four events that same year but endured a series of further operations prior to her death in 1956, aged only 42.

Babe played many exhibition matches, touring America with Gene Sarazen, Bobby Jones, and her good friend Joyce Wethered.

Perhaps it is the fact that she came to golf as a third sporting career that makes her achievement so remarkable. In golf terms her legacy may rest on the determination and courage she showed in winning tournaments despite her illness. This was epitomized by her 1954 win in The US Women's Open championship, one month after surgery for cancer of the colon.

▷**fact**file

- BORN **26th June 1914**
- DIED **27 September 1956**

Major wins:
- 3 X WINNER **The US Women's Open 1948, 1950, 1954**
- 1 X WINNER **The British Ladies Amateur Golf Championship 1947**
- 1 X WINNER **The US Amateur 1947**

What you can learn

It may seem strange to us now, but Babe Zaharias did have to face criticism for her overt strength and fitness which was seen as inappropriate for her gender. Only 5 feet 5 inches she developed her body naturally through all the sports she played, culminating in a physique that was ideal for golf.

Physicality in golf is important though no particular height, weight, flexibility combination is recognized as essential. Tiger Woods is tall—Lorena Ochoa is not. What is true is that you should get fit for golf—not use golf as a means of gaining fitness.

wrist strength and speed to provide the power needed for the impact position

controlled rhythmic movement maintained through the swing

combination of core strength and flexibility to produce controlled rotation

pelvic elasticity required at the top of the swing for change of swing direction

Highlighted are some of the physical attributes of Zaharias that are worth developing for your own game.

developed leg muscles provide support and a stable base for the swing

Arnold Palmer

Arnold Daniel Palmer, sometimes known as the "The King" but universally recognized as "Arnie," is one of the most renowned and acclaimed personalities in the history of professional golf. Notably, he was one of the first stars of televised sport from where he grew his ever-loyal fan base, known affectionately as "Arnie's Army."

With a larger-than-life personality, and great ability as a golfer, Palmer is considered to be one of the most influential factors underpinning the explosion of interest in golf as a spectator sport during the 1960s.

Palmer was born in 1929 in Latrobe, Pennsylvania. He was introduced to golf at a very earlier age by his father, Deacon Palmer, who was the head professional and green-keeper at the nine-hole Latrobe Country Club. At the age of seven Arnie broke 70 at the nearby Bent Creek Country Club.

Palmer attended Wake Forest University with a golf scholarship and, after a brief stint in the US Coastguard, returned to competitive golf, winning the 1954 US Amateur Championship. On his first season on the professional circuit he announced his presence by winning the 1955 Canadian Open. It was his win in the 1958 Masters that started a great run of success. He won 29 tournaments between 1960 and 1963 and won a PGA event every year up to 1970.

American golfing legend Arnold Palmer is besieged by autograph hunters prior to the start of the 110th British Open Golf Championship.

> **fact**file

- BORN **10th September 1929**

Major wins:

- 4 X WINNER **The US Masters 1958, 1960, 1962, 1964**
- 1 X WINNER **The US Open 1960**
- 2 X WINNER **The Open 1961, 1962**
- 1 X WINNER **The US Amateur 1954**
- 1 X WINNER **US Senior Open 1981**
- 2 X WINNER **PGA Senior 1980, 1984**

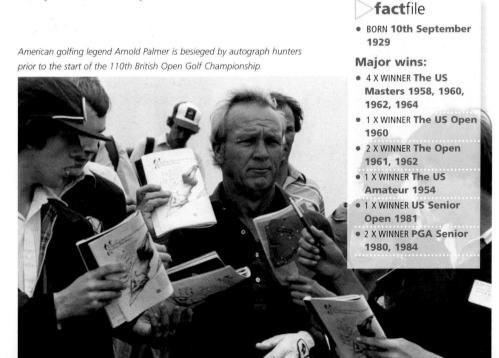

Palmer's reputation was partly based on his risk-taking and aggressive approach to the game. Perhaps one of the reasons he is so loved by his public is the fact that he wore his emotions on his sleeve. He certainly played a part in some of the most memorable finishes to televised tournaments in the history of the sport.

As a player on the Senior PGA Tour, Palmer continued to achieve highly and won ten events on the 1980 Tour, including five senior Majors.

Not only is Palmer a successful golfer but he is also an ambassador for the sport. In a partnership with his agent Mark McCormack he developed an impressive marketing brand and was a successful businessman in his own right. In 1967 he became the first golfing millionaire on the PGA Tour. In October 2006 Palmer retired from professional golf but even then continued to gross an impressive income from his status as an established and much loved sporting personality.

What you can learn

Palmer, in his long career, has witnessed a lot of changes in both the game and the courses. He has even been involved in some of these course changes. One of the biggest changes is the greens, and the greenkeeper's pursuit for perfection. These changes have required the putter heads to evolve. To cope with the faster, smoother greens of today, rather than the slower, coarser greens of yesteryear, the putter heads have had the loft reduced on the putter face.

When considering what putter to use, one of the key factors is the loft of the putter head. Look for between 2 degrees and 4 degrees of loft. The idea of loft is to pick the ball up out of the grass. If the ball is hit with no loft then you will cause the ball to skid over the initial movement. If the ball is helped up by the loft then that initial movement and the rest of the journey is one that sees the ball rolling forward giving it the best possible rolling motion. Choose the loft of the putter to suit the types of greens you play and make—the smoother the greens, the lower the loft.

Figure 1

Figure 2

*A very slight change of putter loft will affect the ball motion as shown in **Figure 1** (which is less lofted) and **Figure 2** (which has a higher loft). You need to inspect the greens before you choose your putter for the round. The practice greens may not always replicate the actual greens.*

Gary Player

Gary Player is one of South Africa's most acclaimed sporting exports and an international golf legend. Born in Johannesburg, Player was awarded the highest honour to be bestowed by the United States Golf Association, receiving the Bob Jones Award in 1966. He was entered into the World Golf Hall of Fame in 1974.

Player showed great promise at aged 14 when, in his first round, he parred the first three holes at his home course at Virginia Park, Johannesburg. He was obviously ambitious and at 16 announced that he would become number one in the world. To realize this ambition he became a professional golfer at the age of 17.

▶ **fact**file

- BORN **1st November 1935**

Major wins:

- 3 X WINNER **US Masters 1961, 1974, 1978**
- 1 X WINNER **The US Open 1965**
- 3 X WINNER **The Open 1959, 1968, 1974**
- 2 X WINNER **US PGA 1962, 1972**
- 3 X WINNER **Senior British Open 1988, 1990, 1997**
- 3 X WINNER **PGA Seniors 1986, 1988, 1990**

Gary Player during the second round of the 2007 ACE Group Classic held at the Quail West Country Club in Naples, Florida.

Player is a family man and during the early part of his career would travel from tournament to tournament with his family in tow. His relentless tournament (and later business) schedule has given Player the unofficial title of the most travelled sportsman. He reckons to have having clocked up nearly 15 million miles during his golfing career.

Player accumulated 24 career titles and played regularly on the US PGA Tour. He held the record for most victories in World Matchplay Championships until he finally lost this title to his fellow South African Ernie Els in 2004. He is the only player to win The British Open in three consecutive decades. Player last won The Masters in 1978 and was the oldest golfer in 1998 to ever make the cut, breaking Sam Snead's record set 25 years earlier.

Player is renowned for his uncompromising drive for perfection. He is a principled man with values that have earned him respect and admiration across the globe. The longevity of Player's career—he was still competing in 2008—is testament to his dedication and commitment to the sport and his stringent regime for health and fitness.

What you can learn

It has been reported that the young Gary Player would practise bunker shots for not hours but for full days. This dedication turned Player into one of the best bunker players ever. This is much the same for the average golfer; get your fundamentals right, practise hard, and success will follow.

In particular Gary Player had great understanding of distance from a greenside bunker. The best way to develop this feel of distance is to play bunker shots to measured distances. Mark three areas out on the green that equally divides the front, middle, and back of the green. Play an equal number of shots to each area (18 balls, six to each area). Once you are able to do this task, try dividing the areas up into six, playing three balls to each.

Always remember the contouring of the green and choose your target accordingly. You will not be aiming to pitch the ball at the pin.

Mentally divide-up the green into three (1, 2, 3) areas as shown above.

Jack Nicklaus

Jack Nicklaus is the holder of some impressive golfing records. His achievements in major tournaments are what set him apart. In 25 years he won 18 Majors (a record in itself) and 73 PGA Tour victories.

Nicklaus, the "Golden Bear" was born in Upper Arlington in Columbus, Ohio on 21st January 1940. He suffered from polio as a child but took to golf quickly. His junior career was impressive, breaking the 70 barrier aged 13 and winning the Ohio State Open three years later. He started as a professional in 1963 and won The Masters and the US PGA Championships, two out of four Majors.

In the golden era of the Nicklaus-Palmer-Player rivalry, the Golden Bear contributed much to establishing the game of golf as a popular spectator sport.

His achievements are numerous. He recorded the lowest-ever score (282 shots) at The US Open for an amateur, and later broke Ben Hogan's record at his second US Open at Baltusrol in 1967 scoring 275 and winning the tournament. In 1978 he eventually accomplished the

triple career Grand Slam, winning all four Major tournaments three times. He was also the first to win two consecutive Masters tournaments (1965 and 1966.) His longstanding tournament record of 271

▷ **fact**file

- BORN **21st January 1940**

Major wins:

- 6 X WINNER **The Masters 1963, 1965, 1966, 1972, 1975, 1986**
- 4 X WINNER **The US Open 1962, 1967, 1972, 1980**
- 3 X WINNER **The Open 1966, 1970, 1978**
- 5 X WINNER **US PGA 1963, 1971, 1973, 1975, 1980**
- 2 X WINNER **The US Amateur 1959, 1961**
- 2 X WINNER **US Senior Open 1991, 1993**
- 1 X WINNER **PGA Senior 1991**

Jack Nicklaus makes his final putt on the 18th green at the 1978 British Open Championship.

achieved at the 1965 Masters was only bettered by Tiger Woods who scored 270 in 1997.

Together with his career highlights Nicklaus has also suffered low times in his career. In the late 1960s Nicklaus was seen to put on weight and lose stamina; this affected his game and he consequently failed to secure a win at any major tournament from 1968 to 1970.

Nicklaus has turned his hand to course architecture, broadcasting and tuition. His book *Golf My Way* is one of the all-time classics of golf.

In 1996 Nicklaus achieved his 100th official career win on the Champions Tour when he won the Tradition for the fourth time. He last appeared at The Masters in 2005 and concluded his professional career at The British Open Championship held at the home of golf, St. Andrews. His last hole culminated in sinking a 15-foot birdie putt prompting a ten-minute standing ovation from the crowd.

Nicklaus is a unique player and the standard by which the greatest players have to measure themselves.

What you can learn

Jack's approach was a masterclass in balance. He could play in a very controlled manner, which allowed him to protect his score. He could also play aggressively, knowing exactly when to go after the birdies. He knew his own game very well. This approach was carried onto the green. Noticeably he would rarely falter over a long putt.

If you can keep a rhythmical and natural stroke you will reduce the pressure of making a long putt. It is easy to tense up on long putts. Keep it natural and spend the time to aim the putt pre-address. Hovering over the putt will only affect your stroke; there is also much greater chance of "manipulation," trying to steer the ball rather than hitting it smoothly and straight.

Trust your stroke, and the practice you have had pre-round, for a good line off the face of the putter.

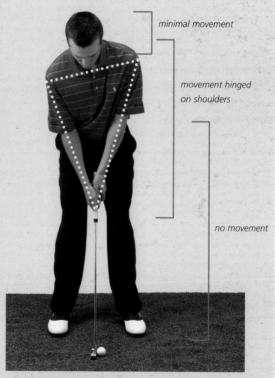

minimal movement

movement hinged on shoulders

no movement

The idea of a pendulum that moves independently is best for visualizing balance, stability, and rhythm.

Nick Faldo

Nick Faldo was a relatively late starter to the game, inspired by watching Jack Nicklaus play the 1971 Masters. Faldo learnt rapidly. A win at the English Amateur Championships a few days after his 18th birthday and the 1975 British Youth Championships set him up for his professional career. He became Britain's youngest Ryder Cup player at the age of 20.

The British public were desperate for Nick Faldo to succeed, given the dominance of the American players over the previous 60 years. Faldo won his first European Tour event in 1977, eventually winning 29 European Tour titles. He is the most successful and prolific Ryder Cup player ever, having represented his team a record 11 times and having clocked up the most points (25) of either team.

However, despite an impressive start to his career, Faldo hit swing problems in the mid 80's. He turned to a then relatively unknown David Leadbetter and remodeled his swing. By 1987 the swing makeover was completed and his performance improved enormously.

Faldo dominated during the late 1980s to mid 1990s winning six Majors including The Masters in 1989, 1990, and 1996. Faldo is

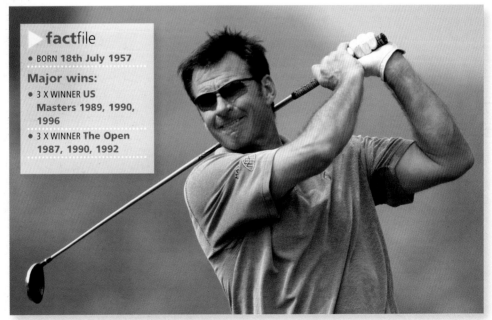

factfile

- BORN **18th July 1957**

Major wins:
- 3 X WINNER **US Masters 1989, 1990, 1996**
- 3 X WINNER **The Open 1987, 1990, 1992**

Nick Faldo plays his tee shot on the 18th hole during the final round of the 2007 UBS Hong Kong Open.

remembered for his remarkable composure, which seemed to unnerve opponents, but not for his charisma.

As the most formidable British golfer of the last 60 years Faldo has been recognized for his contribution and achievements. He was awarded the MBE by the Queen in 1988 and was the 2008 Ryder Cup captain for the European team. Faldo has also been inducted into the World Golf Hall of Fame along with the likes of Sam Snead and Arnold Palmer.

What you can learn

Faldo changed his swing in the early 1980s and, as a result, lost distance. To compensate he set about honing his shot control. With intense practice he knew exactly what club, and what type of shot, would produce the result he needed.

It is important to understand your own game, perfecting what is already great and working on all other aspects to bring them up to the same standard. Nick controlled his shots by understanding the fundamentals of what the club had to do to perform a particular type of shot or distance. You can do the same. In terms of distance, if you need less or more, simply use less or more club. Do not try and get one club to perform a task it very rarely achieves. If you have the wrong club in your hand and try to play a shot half heartedly, or with more aggression, you will change the tension in your body. In turn this will cause unnatural changes to your swing and timing and will reduce your level of consistency. Play what you know… and give yourself confidence.

What I can't control

distance	ground	wind	hazards	state of game
150	soft	still	trees	par to qualify
140	wet	1 club wind	out of bounds	matchplay
130	dry	left to right	lateral water	first hole
120	hard	against	fairway trap	stroke play

the shot

9	draw	chip	set-up
8	fade	drive	time taken
7	straight	pitch	thoughts
6	low	flop	glove
club	**shape of shot**	**type of shot**	**the personal**

What I can control

Annika Sörenstam

Swede Annika Sörenstam announced her retirement from competitive professional golf in 2008 following years of dominance. Winner of 72 LPGA tournaments, including 10 Majors, she scored career earnings of over US$21 million.

Born in Bro near Stockholm, Annika emerged as a major star following her time at VA University of Arizona. She was a product of Sweden's efforts to develop young golfers, something that perhaps led her to open the Annika

Academy at Ginn Reunion Resort in Florida.

Her development saw her change from a shy young junior who, it is rumored, would deliberately three putt to avoid making speeches, to the well-accomplished golfer

▶**fact**file

● BORN **9th October 1970**

Major wins:

● 3 X WINNER **Kraft Nabisco 2001, 2002, 2005**

● 3 X WINNER **LPGA Championship 2003, 2004, 2005**

● 3 X WINNER **The US Women's Open 1995, 1996, 2006**

● 1 X WINNER **The Women's British Open 2003**

● 1 X WINNER **World Amateur Champion 1992**

Annika Sorenstam lines up a putt during day three of the Lexus Cup 2007 at The Vines Resort & Country Club in Perth, Australia.

who tried her hardest to avoid making more than one putt. Prior to her retirement she had publicly announced that she aimed to reach the perfect score of 54 on a par-72 course. She once hit a record-breaking 59 in a LPGA tournament, a card that included a front-nine score of 28.

To date, Sörenstam is without question the best female player of all time and, although she went through a lull during the 2006–7 season due to a neck injury, her start to 2008 suggested she was back to full fitness following her 70th senior win. Ranked second in the world at the time of her retirement (Mexican Lorena Ochoa held the top spot) she certainly retired at the top although many will argue that she quit prematurely.

What you can learn

On her retirement Annika was asked about highlights and, among a few choices, listed her score of 59 in the second round of the 2001 Standard Register Ping LPGA tournament at Moon Valley Country Club in Phoenix, Arizona. She carded 13 birdies, five pars and no bogeys on the 6,459-yard course and admitted to getting a bit nervous towards the end. Ever the competitor however, she also said "it could have been better." Annika missed a 10-foot birdie putt on the 9th (she started her round on the back nine). Annika worked for many years with Swedish coach Pia Nilsson, accompanied by US coach Lynn

Marriott. These two complete game coaches created their Vision54 philosophy. Annika worked with this philosophy of concentrating on the moment and a push for what most would consider impossible—to score 54 on a par-72 round (one-under for every hole).

Few have the ability to turn this dream into reality but everybody can focus on a seemingly impossible target and work toward it. What can you learn? Anything is possible with the necessary skills and the correct mental approach.

12 birdies, (see scores circled in red).   *six pars, (see scores in black)*

Moon Valley Country Club

Hole	1	2	3	4	5	6	7	8	9	Total
Par	4	3	4	5	3	4	4	5	4	36
Score	3	2	3	4	3	4	4	4	4	31

Hole	10	11	12	13	14	15	16	17	18	Total
Par	5	3	4	5	4	3	4	4	4	36
Score	4	2	3	4	3	2	3	3	4	28

| | | | | | | | | | Total | 59 |

Annika's historic card from 2001.

Tiger Woods

It is a rare person who has not heard of Tiger Woods. Born Eldrick Woods in Cypress, California, Tiger was first introduced to the game of golf at the age of two by his late father, Earl. Tiger was a child prodigy when it came to swinging a club. His first television appearance came in 1978 when the three-year-old Tiger appeared on The Mike Douglas Show alongside comedian Bob Hope and demonstrated his potential to the viewing millions.

At eight years old Tiger won his first Junior World Golf Championships; he went on to win six more. From that point on, Tiger honed his skills and rose to fame rapidly. Given the nickname Tiger by his father, he later changed his name officially. At the age of 15 the schoolboy Tiger became the youngest ever US Junior Amateur Champion. In 1994 he won his first major championship, The US Amateur. He is today considered one of the greatest golfers of all time.

> **fact**file

- BORN **30th December 1975**

Major wins:
- 4 X WINNER **The Masters 1997, 2001, 2002, 2005**
- 3 X WINNER **The US Open 2000, 2002, 2008**
- 3 X WINNER **The Open 2000, 2005, 2006**
- 4 X WINNER **US PGA 1999, 2000, 2006, 2007**
- 3 X WINNER **US Amateur 1994, 1995, 1996**

Tiger Woods hits his tee shot on the first hole during the final round of the 2008 Masters Tournament in Augusta, Georgia.

Woods has sustained one of the greatest periods of dominance in men's golfing history. His supremacy since the 1990s owes much to his absolute belief in his abilities. Tiger may experience a couple of "bad days" during a tournament but it would be a foolish player to consider him out of the competition. Tiger has, on numerous occasions, demonstrated that he is the "come-back kid", shooting some spectacular shots to win major events.

Many comparisons can be drawn between Tiger Woods and Jack Nicklaus, and Sam Snead before him. Like these two golfers, Tiger became the third man to win at least five times in three different events on the PGA Tour in any one tournament year (2001) and the only golfer to have achieved this in consecutive years.

In 2007 Tiger matched his 2000 score record achieving a scoring average of 67.79 over the 16 starts.

What you can learn

Although Tiger Woods' game is beyond that of amateur golfers—indeed, it's beyond many professionals too—there is always something we can learn from him. There are numerous facets to his game that are worth emulating such as physical fitness, great swing speed, intense mental focus etc. Another major building block in his game is his confidence. This has grown over the years as he has won major tournaments but we all know, in golf, confidence is a fragile thing. How has Tiger maintained his and what has it meant to him?

Tiger's original mental strength has probably come from having such supportive parents and encouraging coaches. They have always believed in him. When he is playing golf he knows it's the right thing to do and that those around him are right behind him. What relevance does this have for your own game. Simply you will probably play better if you have created the right time and place to play. When you are on the course you should not be worrying about anything other than your next shot.

Tiger's confidence has also helped him in contrasting ways. He has had the mental strength to change his swing. Even when he was at the top of the professional game he believed he could go further and took time out to change his coach and swing. It worked. Yet Tiger also has the strength not to change. If he has a game plan he will stick to it; one bad hole or one bad shot will not deter him. In your game you must believe in what you are doing. Self doubt, especially when standing over the ball is the simplest way to a poor shot.

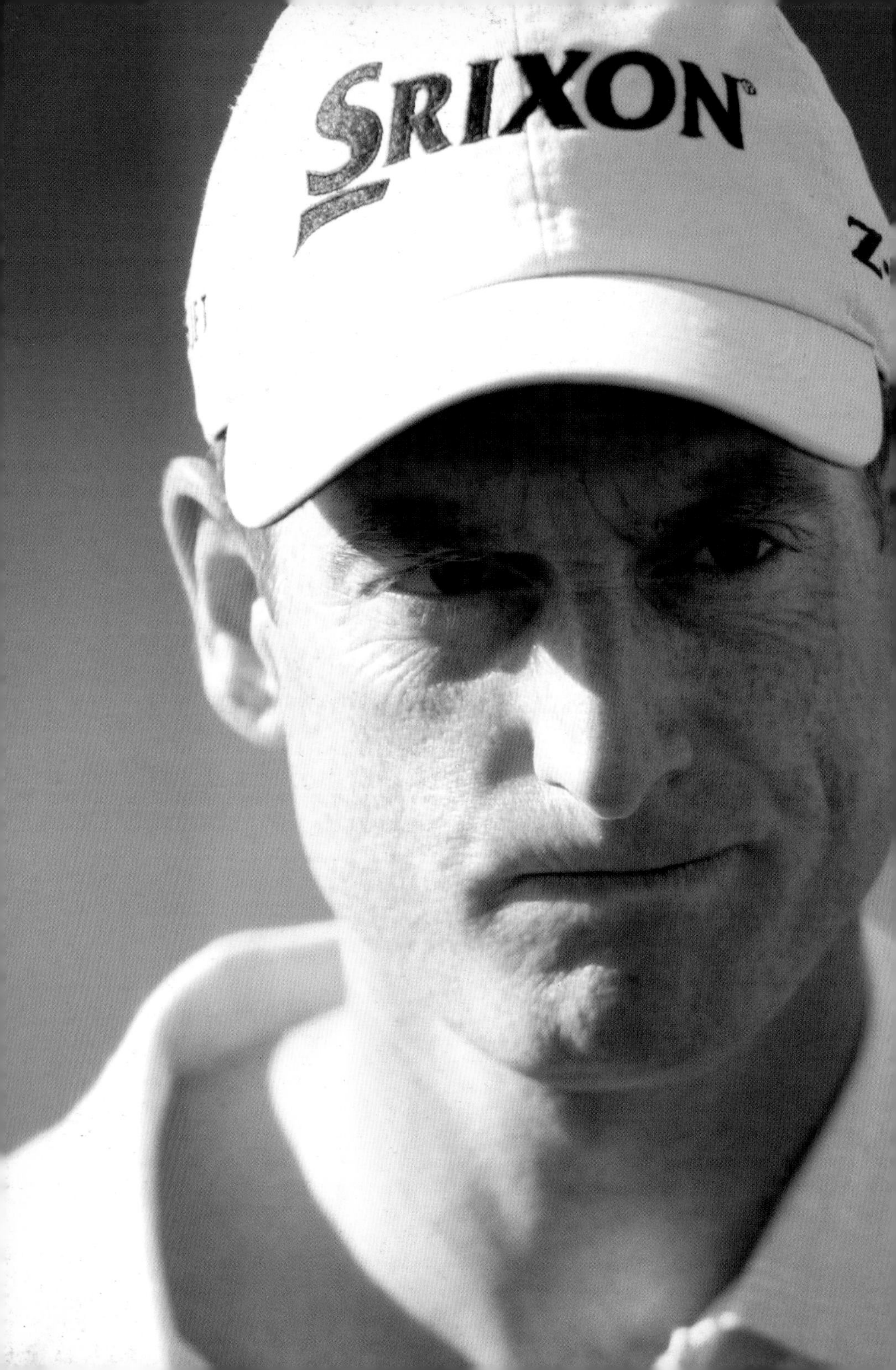
SRIXON

The mind game

Golf is as much a mental as a physical challenge. Perhaps that's why the game is so popular and so endlessly frustrating. One part of your game can be in place while another falls apart. Perhaps the key to the mind game is to understand that fact. Like the physical aspects of golf, you can break the mind game down into small elements, understand them, and work on them.

... mind game?

The mind game in golf is all to do with focus—concentrating on what you should be doing. The focus comes in two parts: immediate focus and goal focus. Both of these facets, if understood correctly, allow you to construct your complete game.

Colin Montgomerie shows his disappointment during the Diageo Championship at Gleneagles, Scotland. The British player is one who has often struggled with focusing on his game; although very successful, commentators have suggested that he could have won more trophies with a more equable approach to golf.

Immediate focus

When you are able to enter your exclusive zone, you have immediate focus. "Being in the zone" is the common phrase now used to describe that moment of producing excellence. In golf this may just be that 30-second period in which you truly have thought out and executed the perfect shot, expertly, from an impossible position. Being in the zone is something all golfers have felt but perhaps never truly understood.

The important thing is to recognize this feeling and incorporate it regularly into your game. Gary Player was once famously described as "lucky" by a spectator. His retort was: "The more I practise, the luckier I get." If you interpret this phrase from Gary Player as meaning: "The more I practise the more I learn how to get into the zone, allowing me to truly focus on what I am trying to achieve," you may understand better that the zone is not some magic place; it's somewhere you will reach more regularly if you pay attention to it.

Having immediate focus is the result of good technique, good decision making, and good play (sometimes good luck, too). You can't force yourself into this zone by any other means than practising purposefully and playing well. Once there, however, you can certainly build on the confidence you gain and the sense of achievement you feel in order to remain in the zone longer and longer.

Goal focus

Your ability to find a reason for what you do and why you do it is your goal focus. Unconsciously your goal focus for golf can leave you searching for something with little understanding of the reasons. It can even lead to questioning why you play golf and to losing all perspective of what you think you actually gain from taking part in the game. Have you ever, in moments of frustration, threatened to leave the golf course never to return again? When you can find your goal focus, you will be much better able to rationalize your feelings and mentally focus on your game for the long haul.

American psychologist Henry Murray from Harvard University suggests in his theory on human motivation that when a goal is reached you will feel a greater need to set higher goals. This increases the emotion to replicate the moment of achievement with a new moment. The more intense the feeling the more drive there is to develop your game… which comes back to practice. It's a positive cycle in action.

Achieve goal

Purposeful practice ⟵ **Set new goal**

A simple positive cycle allows you to keep refreshing your goals. You will move around the cycle more rapidly with limited goals of course.

Motivation

What motivates you? If you analyze your own emotions can you identify the most common aspects of your goal focus in golf? Are they enjoyment for the game, the element of competition, idolization of a person, or is it a way of achieving recognition from others?

Consciously these elements often are not understood; unconsciously, however, they can be the one thing that drives you to fulfill your ambitions. To create an environment that accommodates and reflects these needs has to be the first step in any journey of personal, or golfing, development.

Enjoyment

Understanding your pleasure in the game is key. Which of the following allows you to enjoy golf?

- playing with friends
- playing new golf courses
- winning (money, prizes, acclaim)
- achieving a personal best

- fresh air and scenery
- lowering your handicap
- playing with a new set of clubs.

First identify with the items in the list above. Then remember them as reasons why you relish a game of golf. It is important to increase your sense of well-being when playing new courses, using a new piece of equipment, or simply walking in the fresh air.

Also, of course, you can begin to create environments that you are comfortable with. If you derive pleasure from playing with friends, then try to play with friends that will make you feel at ease and comfortable. If you want to win that prize, set your practice program accordingly.

justification of fitted clubs

more enjoyment

enjoyment from using them

results improve

wanting them to perform well

more practice and care taken

Another positive "cycle" but one that feeds into the enjoyment of buying equipment and benefiting from using it. Golf lends itself to technical development and you may enjoy keeping up with the latest; this may be good for your game both mentally and technically.

This last point is a more difficult one. You can (money and time allowing) go and play a new course but you can't always win. When setting targets, it is essential not to be too greedy. If you want to beat a lowest score do not say by how much you intend to beat it. If your lowest score is 90 then break 90, do not state that you intend to shoot 86. This only creates a pressure gap of no man's land, a place into which you have not yet ventured.

Playing for enjoyment also brings rewards. You may treasure a new set of clubs, and the club change offers you a new reason for wanting them to work, which they often do. If you can find the right fitted clubs from the start then you are more likely to trust fully in what this new set offers you and your game. Work the positive thoughts together. There is, too, the bonus of seeing the new clubs (seemingly) bring rewards.

Lessen the pressure

With a previous personal best of 87 on the same course, why add needless pressure when coming down the 15th and all you need do is shoot two over on the last four holes to finish with your 86 shots? If you have a game plan to shoot 86 then when, on the last four holes, you make a double bogey you are doubling the pressure and sense of disappointment. It is when pressure increases that it becomes even harder to chase your target. There is also the unconscious confusion of now changing your game plan, and this often takes time to mentally adjust.

6	5	403	4	380	
7	4	373	4	360	1
8	3	212	3	191	1
9	5	384	4	364	5
		3412	36	3220	
10	4	434	4	410	1
11	4	395	4	371	8
12	6	527	5	514	2
13	5	310	4	295	1
14	3	149	3	135	

Competition

The element of conflict will be what drives many golfers, frequently those who have come from other sports. This association with competition often comes from previous successes which may not always represent the same activity as the current focus. You may like the feeling of winning in business so you want to win in golf too. Regardless, there is still a need to want to recreate the feeling. The feeling is actually not only about the success but also about the journey you go through when developing your golf game. Any achievement only demonstrates an end of a journey, allowing you to reflect on where you have come from.

When focusing on achievement make sure you give value to the journey you have been through—and are still on—and not just to the pleasure of the moment.

Idolization

Two powerful elements of goal focus in golf are hero worship and the need for appreciation, not only by fellow golfers but also by the non-golfing community.

Idolization

As a boy Tiger Woods idolized Jack Nicklaus. Nicklaus' achievements are now being matched by Woods. Just because the latter may surpass the achievements of his idol it does not detract from the respect one great player holds for another. Woods now has a deeper understanding of, and mutual respect for, the journey taken by Nicklaus as he progressed

through the ranks as a golfer. This journey for Woods adds value to the mystery he once had when he watched Nicklaus dominate the game, thereby adding value and association with every achievement he makes.

Having an idol can be a way to measure your own achievements. Identification with them, overtly or in private, can help you discuss and review your own game. You may

Tiger Woods speaks during a press conference as the Tiger Woods Foundation announces the New AT&T National Tournament at the National Press Club in Washington. Tiger has learned to build on the admiration that others have for him in a positive way. He thrives on it. As well as "idolizing" Tiger you can also learn to accept praise and build on it.

never win any Majors, but you might be able to match your own development in tandem with one of the greats. Emulation of greatness can never be bad.

Recognition

Recognition can also play a large part in the enjoyment you derive from golf. You may have been given praise your whole life. Such feedback reassures you that what you do is appreciated by others. If you acknowledge any form of praise it is clear that this acknowledgment is important to your success and therefore has value.

This feel-good factor does not always come from an outside source; it can come from you directly. Whatever its source, to feel good about what you are doing is healthy in life and on the golf course. Value yourself, praise yourself, and value those who offer you praise because it will no doubt be deserved.

Bigger than yourself

Many people, and you may be included in this number, will find something in their lives that allows them to feel that they are part of a greater purpose… something that offers them meaning. For the young this could be something like their college football team; for the older generation it may be a military unit, the family, or the workplace.

Whatever the source, it will have value because it was something they could be part of; it offered opportunity and purpose. For a golfer this could represent nationality, a golf club, a college team, even a Ryder Cup team. These are all important and represent something that should be a joy to those involved.

If you can find something that you can represent on the golf course and in life, something that gives you pride, this makes you answerable to something other than yourself. You only have to look again at Tiger Woods to understand this.

Woods represents a brand, not that of a sports company but the Tiger Woods brand. Here is a man who has a whole world of expectation on his shoulders to perform, on and off the course. This could be a pressure for Woods but he has been able to develop this into a positive feeling. If he represents his brand known as Tiger Woods in the best possible light then there is no reason for anyone to criticize what he does.

The brand that is Tiger Woods is not about the money he can make. It is about the millions of people that also look up to and respect him and what he represents. This is how role models are created. From the first thing in the morning till last thing at night, how Woods chooses to represent himself does not just affect him; it influences his family, friends, sponsors, and spectators. This would be no different from a young child looking up to their parents. Every action that is made by that parent reinforces the child's outlook on life.

Be proud of your brand, and remember— whatever you do—your individual action may not affect you personally but it will most certainly affect your brand. This should give you meaning and purpose.

Your approach

Create some time for yourself and look analytically at your game and your approach to golf. Initially, grade yourself on how committed you are to the development of each area of your game, both on the physical and psychological sides. Then spend five minutes, honestly, completing the technical, physical, and mental charts below.

How did you fare? There is no right or wrong score, just the opportunity to see where you might improve. Do you spend more time on one aspect (mind/body) of the game than the other? Don't worry about this, but in future try to blend the aspects of the game into one. When you are practising or playing golf you are constantly combining both mental and physical challenges. One complements the other—one harms the other.

Books, DVDs, and teachers will give you the tools to work on each of these areas, but you need to be the one that creates a routine to accommodate each of these into your golfing life.

Flexible and focused attitude

When working through each area of your game, a flexible and focused approach will help you develop effectively. Be flexible because, in today's busy world it is often hard to set structures firmly in place. You can often face distractions that can affect your routine. Try to be responsive when tackling any areas of

Key

1 = have never worked on

2 = have very rarely worked on

3 = have worked on once a week

4 = have worked on every other day

5 = have worked on most days without fail

Technical	1	2	3	4	5
Putting					
Short game					
Bunker game					
Short irons					
Mid irons					
Long irons					
Woods					
Driver					

Your average score (if you scored 8 x 3) for the technical area = 24. Your actual score =

Physical	1	2	3	4	5
Aerobic endurance					
Muscular endurance					
Muscular strength					
Flexibility, mobility					
Diet and hydration					

Your average score (if you scored 5 x 3) for the physical area = 15. Your actual score =

Mental	1	2	3	4	5
Goal setting					
Pre-round preparation					
Relaxation					
Pre-round practice					
Course management					
Pre-shot routine					
Visualization					
Forgetting a bad shot					

Your average score (if you scored 8 x 3) for the mental area = 24. Your actual score =

your game. When you structure any personal development regime, whether it is diet, fitness, study or just putting, there is a danger that you are setting up the possibility of failure, especially if the routine is too strict. Flexibility should allow for change, making the daily tasks more realistic and achievable. In simple terms, try not to beat yourself up just because you have failed to do one of your pre-set tasks. Also, be focused in your learning and, importantly, slow down. Spending 30 minutes hitting only ten balls in a focused manner is far better than hitting 50 balls in the same time. This gives your brain the chance to concentrate and to play with a relaxed state of mind—the ideal emotion to take on the course. These purposeful shots will allow you to enjoy the learning process.

Focus also by finding out what matters and fix on this rather than the things that do not require your time. Most golfers will spend 80 percent or more of their time working on their swing. This is a strange decision bearing in mind that there are more than 20 different areas of the game that need attention. Focus your efforts in an efficient manner, and your efforts will not go to waste. And when you get the chance to reflect on a round, check out and praise yourself when the results of your target are rewarded.

Off-course practice

Everybody recognizes that golf is about more than just swinging a club. Players on the various professional tours surround themselves with a team of experts in different fields. Such a team may include a nutritionist, psychologist, putting coach, swing coach, fitness instructors, and club-build specialists as well as a management team and even a life coach! You too will play better golf if you receive suitable help.

Support in your lessons

Naturally you will realize that you cannot always achieve what you want without the help of others, so it is important that you find the very best support. This comes from choosing the right type of people. Realistically you will be focusing on one golf skills coach, somebody with expertise in the all-round game. If you have the resources think further afield; try a nutritionist, fitness coach, maybe a putting coach, each to concentrate on one aspect of your development.

Importantly choose experts and listen to their recommendations. Talk to the person before embarking on any routine. Whoever it is, if you are embarking on a series of sessions, consider the following.

- Will you enjoy a style of instruction that suits your learning needs? You may prefer to learn primarily in a verbal or visual way. Find out the style of teaching offered by your instructor before committing to any long-term program. It is important to understand what is being said to you when you wish to learn. If you are a visual learner your instruction should offer lots of images, demonstrations, or video analysis. If you are a verbal learner you will benefit from descriptive instruction. Motor skill learners need the practical involvement of the tuition, having hands-on experience, and learning from the feeling of things. Find what learning method you prefer, even if it is a mix of these styles, as this will allow you to absorb the information faster.

- All coaches should want to know you and what you want from the sessions. This will give you both a better understanding of your goals focus and will create a mutual understanding between coach and client. Most good coaches will start with a questionnaire to establish this information and should always refer to this document to ensure targets are being met during any future sessions.

- Every session should start with an evaluation of the previous session and should have a clear strategy for what needs to be done during the current session, allowing you, the client, to understand what is being asked of you. Try to enforce this or ask questions related to what you have done between sessions. Show or describe what you have been taught; this will allow the coach to reinforce or correct you, which is often needed between sessions.

- Every session should be carried out in an environment that allows you to feel at ease. For example, you may be anxious about working on the range in front of others. Discuss this with the coach with a view to arranging a different venue and to working on your fear.
- Finally remember that learning is a two-way street. Static receipt of information is unlikely to help you much. You need to feel confident about discussing your game, and you should also put as much into practice and learning as into your playing.

Support during practice

As well as establishing a focused environment within your lesson, it is also important to have the right frame of mind when practising. Both lessons and practice should be done with a purpose. Golf is a game that has to be completed in the fewest amounts of shots; this is the purpose of the game. If you decide to practise, then you are making a conscious choice to improve. Give your practice the same purpose that the game asks of you. Practise as you would play a game, that is, with total focus, aiming for great shots.

Phil Mickelson talks to his coach Butch Harmon during the second day of previews before the U.S. Open at Torrey Pines. You need to trust and respect your coach but having the confidence to talk to him and share ideas and anxieties are also key. It needs to be a two-way relationship.

Manage your game 1

It is important to have optimum control of your game, and to have a system that is programed into your mind is the best weapon for looking after your own game. The mnemonic CARVE has been created for just this.

CARVE

Carve comprises all the tools needed for your mind to start guiding your actions on the course:

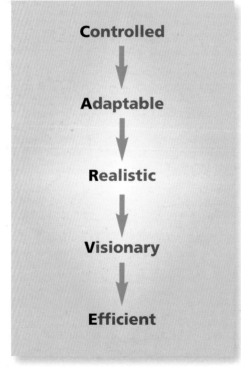

Controlled

↓

Adaptable

↓

Realistic

↓

Visionary

↓

Efficient

This mnemonic can also be implemented in your daily work or domestic routines and if set up with good understanding it will prove a great asset.

Controlled

This is the ability to look after your own decisions and to take action at the right times. In one round of golf if you are an average mid-handicap player you will spend only 45 minutes of total focus on your game, and this is how it should be. To spend a full round concentrating on the golf will not be time best spent.

Whether on the course or practising, never try to focus for too long. It is important to allow the brain to relax and give yourself time to recover before the next shot. This turning on and off has to be done with a degree of control, which is why it is essential to have a trigger for the start of a game or task, and a second one to acknowledge the finish of the game or task. Most sports offer this, but golf does not. Unlike a sprinter hearing the sound of the starter, which denotes the time for moving into position, a golfer has no indicator to associate that it is time to play the shot.

The time line (next page) shows the process of focus and routine for the golfer and sprinter and indicates where best to have your triggers.

The comparison is made with the sprinter because we associate this sport with a series of definitive steps from walking out onto the track up to the moment of the gun going off.

Preparation zone

Entering the preparation zone in sport allows you time to get psychologically and physically ready. You should not reflect on the past or anything behind you, only what lies ahead. Like a golfer, a sprinter will often chat to other runners as they enter the arena and move onto the track but the moment the kit bag is put down behind the lane the conversation should stop and the preparation start. This is a good technique for a golfer.

The preparation zone needs a trigger that tells you it is time to focus on the job at hand. Try to concentrate on an imaginary line known as the play line. Once you have crossed it, the time has come to commit.

Your trigger, which could be the tap of the golf club on the ground or the tightening of the glove, should follow after you have done all your preparation. Establish a routine over which you have complete control and develop it into a habit. It will allow the unconscious to know what you are about to do. Your routine should be used in practice and on the golf course at every opportunity. If you teach your mind a routine, you will reinforce every shot with a check list. A good routine/check list will never leave out any important preparation.

	Track runner	Golfer
Enter the preparation zone	1. putting the kit bag down	putting the golf bag to rest
	2. setting out the starting block	selecting shot and club for the situation
	3. loosening off and stretching	loosening off with a few gentle swings
	4. visualizing the race and the finish	visualizing the ball flight and target
	5. feeling the start out (often short burst forward)	making the practice swing needed
On your marks	6. settling into the blocks	settling down into your set-up
Get set	7. focus on what is about to come	focus on the target of aim
Go	8. start running, settling into a relaxed sprint	swing the club in a relaxed movement

Manage your game 2

Adaptable

To be adaptable in golf you need to be able to play any shot humanly possible for any situation. You probably have a game plan as to how you would like to play a golf hole (e.g. you must hit the ball 240 yards down the middle), yet this can often lead to disappointment when you cannot actually execute the planned shot. Much as you would like to know what is going to happen, you must adapt to what could actually happen. Reading the conditions of the course and weather from one day to the next could require completely different shots or clubs. Sometimes you may feel pressured to reach a par 4 in two shots, but why force it when you know there are difficult weather conditions or some other factor that will not allow you to get there. The tension will cause a negative result. If you have to take three shots into a par 4 then make them count and minimize any risk. This will reduce any stress and will allow you to make better choices.

Realistic

Sometimes you have to make a golfing decision that may put you into more trouble. For example, you are in the rough behind a bunker. Do you come out sideways or take on the trap? Or, you have 175 yards to the green over water; do you go for the green or lay up?

Naturally you will look at the potential results of your shot... the positive and negative. Also you will take in account the overall game situation, whether you are going for a good score for the round or looking at winning or losing a hole in match play.

When faced with this kind of situation, how do you make a sensible decision based on realistic evidence? Last time you faced a similar situation, what happened? A simple formula can help you build up a realisitc view of your game and take away the mental pressure.

Decide your ideal outcome and note how hard the shot is. Think also about the last time you had a similar shot; were you lucky with the outcome or did you make, with hindsight, a stupid decision?

On the course
How hard is the shot?

Very easy		1	2	3	4	5	6	7	8	9	10	Very hard

How serious is it if I miss?

Not that vital	1	2	3	4	5	6	7	8	9	10	Critical

After the round
Did I make a god decision?

Very poor		1	2	3	4	5	6	7	8	9	10	Very good

Did I hit a good shot?

Very poor		1	2	3	4	5	6	7	8	9	10	Very good

Look at the table (on previous page). Have something like this in your mind. Check the appropriate number. If it is below seven then commit to the shot. Your decision should be easy if you're being realistic with yourself. Make that decision, play the shot and later, when the round is finished, analyse how you would play that shot again. After the round you are looking for scores of seven and over.

Overall this should encourage you to be reaslitic about your game.

Visionary

A visionary has a focus and belief in themself. Any golfer who can add creativity into their game will add to their repertoire on the golf course. Just because you may hit a 7 iron 150 yards, why not break with tradition and try to knock down a 5 wood for the same distance, or putt from five to ten yards off the green? If you can see the shot in your mind then you will learn to play the game with your subconscious.

Efficient

This plays an enormous part in all aspects of golf. The more ready you are, then the less chance there is for you to be caught off guard.

Calculate all possible outcomes that could occur on the golf course. This could include change of weather (have the right clothes) or playing into wind (practise your low shot). Whatever the situation it is important to be efficient. Your preparation should always include the following:

- checking your bag for the required tools for the day
- practising all areas of your game before stepping onto the golf course
- allowing yourself plenty of time to get ready
- arriving on the course focused on the reason you are there, in order to give yourself time to relax; then play with purpose.

Do not be dictated to by greens or fairways in regulation. Play each shot as you find it and look for the best result from there. The mnemonic CARVE gives you a system to manage each shot and stay within the moment. Take your time to arrive at the golf course and be comfortable with being there. The golf course should be a place where you can escape the hustle and bustle of life.

And if it all goes wrong? Take the drop (as Ross Fisher of England did in the $5m USD HSBC Champions tournament in Shanghai) and put it behind you. Focus solely on the next shot.

Putting

You may love the game because of the challenge faced by hitting a small ball over a great distance to a given target. However, the "distance" game is less than 40 percent of what is required of you within your game of golf. The remaining game is one of precision and accuracy... in which putting plays a large part.

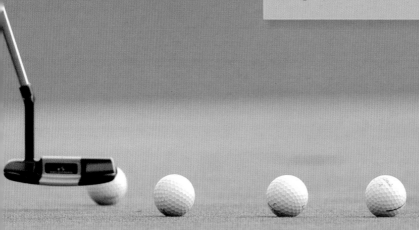

Thinking about basics

Putting is described as a "game within a game" by a number of our great golfers—and for good reason. The approach, skill, and mental focus are completely different to that which is required for the "distance" game. Putting requires a similar approach to that adopted by snooker or pool players: one of precision, accuracy, and above all patience.

Natural, instinctive...

To an extent, the skill of putting should be a natural and instinctive experience. However, as most golfers will contest, this is difficult to achieve. As with anything, practice leads to improvement. Like driving a car, the experience will eventually become a natural and almost subconscious one. But also like driving a car, you do not want to "learn" bad habits!

Robert Karlsson of Sweden hits a putt on the 13th green during the final round of the 108th US Open at the Torrey Pines Golf Course. His classic putting style is a model of consistency. His head only moves long after the ball has left the putter face.

... and consistent

To achieve a natural and instinctive experience when putting you must develop consistency in the putting stroke. It is the consistency of your stroke that will lead to that experience—your muscles memorizing the movement and registering this for the next time. A repeatable putting stroke will eventually enable you to putt in the exact direction you are aiming for. If this is achieved then it will not be the putting stroke that takes you off target but your errors in the reading of the contours on the green.

There is no set rule for how the putter should be held or how you should set-up for the putt as long as you are off to one side of the ball and not behind it. Putting should be something that is natural and comfortable, which allows you to be more instinctive in your approach. Putting is about "the feel of the stroke."

You and your putter

Unfortunately, manufacturers have largely dictated how you should be set-up when putting by building standard putters, admittedly of different types (see page 138), to fit all. However, people are not created the same; they have differences in height, weight, posture, and stance. Often a standard manufactured putter will inhibit the extent of any benefit you could gain from lessons from your golf professional. You find yourself unable to repeat their tips on the putting fundamentals because you do not have the right tools for the job. Either the putter sets you into a negative position (e.g. brings your hands too far out, makes you stand too tall or too short, or does not allow for your hands to move forward of the ball), or you putt the ball in a negative manner (pushing the ball out, or aiming off target).

Many golf professionals will tell you that your eyes should be directly of the ball when putting; this is not necessarily true in every case. When set up with the correct stance and posture the position of the eyes is controlled mainly by the shoulders. The shoulder pivot point to the centre of the eyes will dictate this position. As a general guide the

longer the neck the more the eyes should be outside the ball and vice versa the shorter the neck the more the eyes should be inside the ball.

Set yourself up at the correct angles: back tilted, legs relaxed, relatively tall. Go through your putting routine... then choose your putter.

The set-up

As with any shot in the game of golf, your set-up is fundamental to achieving a successful shot. Do you keep your feet and shoulders square to the target? Do you have your eyes over the ball? How do you grip the club? Is the putter address central or on your front foot? These are all good questions that are not easy to answer. The first thing to learn is you should not be in a position dictated by the putter. Your body shape, size, posture, weight, and dynamics will influence how you should set up for a successful putting stroke.

Start with the grip

There are many types of putting grips today but the right grip for you is the one that helps you with your set-up and stroke. It will also be the one you feel most confident with. Probably the last thing you want to change is your putting grip but it is worth going back to basics for a moment to see if there is scope of change—and potential for more consistent putting.

Get into what feels like the most comfortable and stable pose—without your putter. Adopt the following sequence:
- relax
- ensure your feet are parallel to each other
- keep your weight evenly balanced
- bend your knees very slightly
- hold your back straight tilting it forward from your hips
- let your arms naturally hang down from your shoulders.

Build from here, with your club in your hand this time. Then drop the putter and press the palms of your hands together.

Take the posture as on the previous page and let your hands drop, palms together. Make sure they are making a straight line down to the ball.

Different grips

Once settled into this posture you can grip the club again. Start with your natural grip, then try some variations. Three are shown here. Try putting some balls with each grip. Notice any difference? Feel more confident with one particular style? It's up to you. Each grip has its own plus points but no one grip is perfect for a standard putter. Any of these grips can be adapted to suit the belly or broom handle putter, but with the broom handle putter you should separate your hands to gain more control. Often this will suit those with the yips.

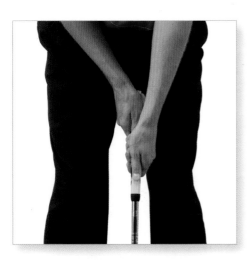

These styles are three of many. You can experiment. In general, always hold the club lightly and don't forget that its grip can be different shapes and sizes (see page 141).

1. The crossover grip puts your hands the wrong way round. Players who prefer this say it makes the right hand less dominant. A dominant right hand often leads to a pulled putt.

2. The claw grip is adopted by those who enjoy the extra control they feel from just two fingers placed on the shaft.

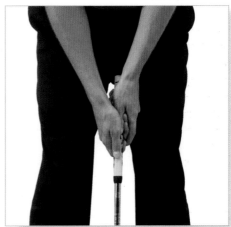

3. The natural grip largely emulates the overlapping grip used in the swing.

The stroke

Your main aim is to hit the ball on a straight line... and into the hole. Despite different borrows on different greens, you are trying to hit the ball along an imaginary straight line. It will be the shape of the green that makes the ball move off this line, not your shot. The putter is the tool you are using to strike the ball—the stroke. How your body moves in playing the shot is important—your movement dynamics. And the movement of the ball is also vital—the roll or ball motion.

The stroke

The ball should be hit with the centre of the face allowing for maximum sweet spot and feel. If you address the ball in the middle then you should find it easier to return to that same position.

The next key tip is to have the putter shaft as near vertical as possible.

Always keep your putter flat, neither toe up nor toe down.

You always aim in a straight line—never try to "shape" a putt. It is the contours of the green that will cause your ball to roll off line and toward your target.

Try not to move too far away from a vertical position; this will maintain the true loft of the putter. And return the putter at impact to this same vertical point for a better roll of the ball.

The ideal stroke of the putt, is to move the putter head one thirds back and two thirds through. Perfect this on the practice green so it is second nature on the course; don't try to consciously count the "thirds" when putting in a competition.

one third

two thirds

Extra pair of eyes

Rocco Mediate and his caddie line up a shot on the 17th green, in the fourth round of the 108th US Open golf tournament in which Mediate was eventually to lose in a play-off. His green reading was great and it's no doubt that having an extra pair of eyes helped.

Movement dynamics

Importantly, and this may be contrary to what you are used to thinking, the putting stroke path has to be in an arc, not straight back and through. This is because the putting movement should come from the shoulders. If you adopt the correct stance and posture and aim to pull back in a straight line, your natural movement will see the shoulders move inside the line on the back stroke and the same after the follow through, following impact.

To demonstrate this, place the palms of your hands flat together; then make the same swing movement as a baseball player, then the same movements as a golfer putting. You will notice that your body moves in an arc much like the baseball swing.

It would be wrong to believe you can keep the path of the putter totally square during a putting stroke; this is clearly unnatural and will only cause tension in your body,—your shoulders move—something we want to avoid.

It is possible, however, to start from a square position, address the ball, and move back to a square address position through impact.

Natural stroke

The more natural the stroke, the more chance you have of returning to that same square position through impact. As you have probably noticed this means the putting stroke is an arc; an arc that rotates around your body.

- Your legs do not move—this will cause you to sway off the correct line.
- Your head does not move—where your head goes your body goes.
- Your hands do not move—they keep the face square to that of the putter path.

The classic pendulum of the swing. Only your head must be completely still until well after impact.

When the putter returns to the start point the face of the putter will be square to the path of the ball.

In practising and perfecting your shot, note how the body creates this slight rotation. The curvature is only very minor as you can see in the photographs with the putting mirror. The longer the putt, the more the rotation will be noticed. The absolute key is repeatability.

Set up with everything (club, feet, head, hands etc.) aligned. Keep the putter shaft parallel and vertical to the ball with the head square to the target.

When taking the putter back follow the natural path dictated to by the shoulders; this will see you come inside your line naturally.

Through impact the head and putter path should have returned to the ball square. After impact the putter path will again naturally come inside the line following the course set by the shoulders.

Ball motion

With your set-up completed, and movement dynamics understood, you need to turn your attention to the motion of the ball. The key starting point is to remember that if you create the correct motion in your putt, the ball will travel in a straight line. When reading greens and calculating the breaks within each green it is important to understand that your aim point should run in a straight line from your starting point.

The strike and ball motion

Once you have found your intended path, the putter head should sit square and the shaft near-vertical at address and should be the same at impact. It is essential that the ball is hit as near to the centre point of the putter face as possible; this will give you the best chance of feel. With the shaft angle correct, the putter head should be angled upward through the impact phase.

The ball at rest

When a ball is at rest on the green it will often nestle down into its own grassy bed. It is important to ensure that the putter not only lifts the ball out of the resting position but also creates a forward motion that allows the ball to roll over the green surface.

The ball will jump or skip across the green if it is not lifted out of its own grassy bed; also, if the ball is hit with reverse rotation it will skid and come to rest a lot quicker.

If you position your hands too far forward of the club head this will cause you to reduce the loft on the club face and so prevent the club lifting the ball up out of the grass with forward spin.

Using technology

Many professionals can now access monitoring equipment to look at your putting. The printout from such machines can help you fine-tune your stroke. The aim is always to produce a natural and repeatable stroke.

Image **A** shows electronic analysis of the ball stike during putting. This application of technology replaces the old version of taping over the club face, allowing you to see where on the putter's face you are actually striking the ball.

Image **B** monitors the angle of the putter head rotation during the stroke. The putter head rotation comes from the putter path which is created by your shoulders; this should not come from the rotation of your hands.

Image **C** demonstrates the putter face angle during the putter path. If you start with the face open or closed then you are more likely to return the putter face at impact in the same position. This will make you question your stroke resulting in changes to the wrong thing. Start the face square and this will increase your ability to stay square through impact.

Image **D** shows that it is possible also to measure the rhythm of the stroke whether more speed is being generated before or after ball contact.

A

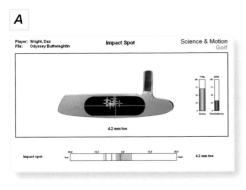

C

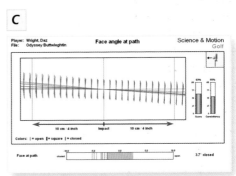

B

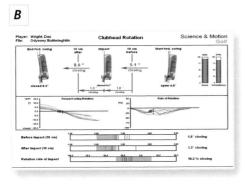

D

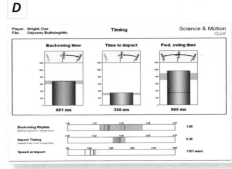

The perfect putt

A putt is perfect if it goes in the hole. You will not, sadly, be able to do this every time. What you need to look for is a good routine that enables you to repeat the natural stroke and to find the hole, as often as possible.

Approach the green knowing that you will set-up and strike correctly. With these elements of your game understood, think about the whole sequence of perfect putting:

- **set-up**—stance and alignment
- **observation**—reading the contours and pace of the green
- **focus**—being in the right frame of mind

- **stroke**—the result of both good technique and feel
- **celebration**—a necessary part of building a winning mentality.

Observation

When reading a green it is important to assess and appreciate the contours, condition, and

Celebration

Celebration should always play a large part in your putting game as this has a positive emotional effect for the future. You don't need to go overboard but positive celebration allows you to create a positive emotion about such a difficult task.

One of the great golf coaches of the twentieth century, Harvey Pinnick, has always said that every player should "hole out" because by not doing so they will develop a fear of certain putts and cause a lack of both experience and confidence. Today's young golfing hopefuls will often be seen playing various putting games which are played more for amusement than for practice but they do allow them to putt the impossible putt or hole out to win the hole or bet.

The more putts you hole, in practice and in matches, and the more you celebrate the great putts, the more you will gain in confidence. Your memory will be re-enforced and you will be left with a lasting feeling of just what you can achieve… just what is possible.

Anthony Kim celebrates as he holes a birdie putt on the 18th green during the third round of the Wachovia Championship.

features of the surrounding area as this will dictate how the ball will travel across the green. It is a clever course architect who creates a green that appears to contour one way but will actually roll the ball in the opposite direction.

This architectural mischief is often created by a designer who has a real appreciation of the natural lie of the land and who is then able to build a green that casts an illusion, fooling the golfer into thinking the green works contrary to what it is actually doing. This certainly makes for a more interesting, if not more frustrating game—all the fun of the challenge!

In this situation, the architect becomes your "enemy." To combat your enemy you must get into their mind and challenge what they have created. To do this you must strip away the illusion and bring back your appreciation of the natural lay of the land. In this situation your eyes are often the biggest deceiver so you must call upon other things to make sense of the situation. It is a good idea to first observe the hole from the lowest point, then from where your ball lies in direct line of the flag and then slowly walk up one side of that line, coming back the opposite side. This will allow you to feel the lie of the land with your feet, confirming or challenging what you have visually assessed from the line of travel. It will also enable you to focus upon what the contours are actually doing around the green— not what you see them doing. Do not be afraid to reassess this if you are not sure.

Regarding the pace of the green, observation is your only tool. Remember, you must:

- **practise beforehand**—hoping that the practice green is the same pace as the actual greens

- **watch other players putt**—and don't offer to go out of turn, always let others putt first if at all possible
- **take every opportunity to putt**—putting out even if you don't need to (e.g. in match play) and having practice putts if time and the rules permit.

If you are striking the ball with confidence you will soon build the correct pace into your stroke. It will be a matter of feel.

Feel and rhythm

To develop a "feel" for a green it is important to first have a consistent, rhythmical, and natural stroke. Your stroke should be as described earlier: one third back, two thirds through. By taking it two thirds through will not allow the putter the chance to slow within the stroke. A slowing putter head will often leave the putt short. The best rhythm to have is that of an even-paced stroke, without any erratic or uncontrolled movements. "Feel" is something that is developed over time, having regularly practised a rhythmic swing over different distances.

Focus

The very last thought before making a putting stroke should be concentrated on the back of the hole. This should be the only thought in your head. A good exercise is to find and focus upon a distinctive blade of grass or a slightly different shade of mud positioned at the back of the hole, or a mark or a bit of writing on the cup. This target should be established before your set-up and again once set-up. You should have one last glance at that target and then let everything else just happen, trusting your stroke mechanics.

The Short Game

Getting up and down from near to the green is not just important for good scoring—it's fundamental. And it is in the short game that the great players stand out. To master the short game requires a lot more than just good technique. It needs careful thought and considerable feel. The good news? You can do it.

Use your imagination

Movement dynamics are nearly always the same in the short game, regardless of the length of the shot. In this, the short game is similar to putting. Repeatability is the key: same swing, just different golf clubs allowing you to hit different distances.

Left handed Phil Mickelson playing a chip shot with an open club face and feet close together. He has taken his glove off for extra feel.

The short game, however, requires lots of variety and imagination from you, the golfer. You only have to look at the likes of Tiger Woods or Gary Player to appreciate this. Much like these two great golfers you have to be prepared to use your own ideas to create the best possible results from your short game. In order to do this you need to understand the basic fundamentals of this part of the game, starting with the vocabulary.

Some golfers do get in a muddle about the names of the shots. Knowing the right name isn't critical—but it can be a problem if you then confuse the associated techniques. Try to think in terms of:

- pitch shot
- chip shot
- bump and run shot
- lob shot.

Each of the above is generally associated with a certain distance, club, and course type. But there are many overlaps. You can chip from any distance, bump and run with more than one type of club, and use your lob shot with a variety of greens. However, you need to be able to:

- expand your repertoire—knowing how to play each kind of shot in a range of conditions
- limit your options—so that you can play your shot with confidence.

This latter point is important. The short game depends very much on touch, which is varied for each shot. You can't return readily to a repeatable swing. Thus a confident shot is crucial. Lack of confidence can often mean you hurry through with a shot and hit it thin, or nervously pull back on a shot and hit it fat.

Short game principles

These are general guidelines for when each shot should be played. Crucially only make the decision on the day, as you stand over the ball. Don't decide before you have given the shot plenty of thought.

Target—what exactly is your number one target and where else would be acceptable?

Weather—is the wind, standing water, rain etc. going to affect the shot?

Green—is it holding or firm, sloping or flat?

Hazards—what is in your line of shot, how much do you need to avoid it/them?

Clubs in your bag—do you have the wedge you ideally need for the shot?

State of play—are you doing well in a strokeplay competition; playing a matchplay shot; are you confident etc?

Take your time—weigh up all the possible options and outcomes, then cross the line and commit.

Save a shot

Think about the course you are playing before choosing your clubs. You may decide to take more or fewer wedges depending on the type of fairways and greens you are likely to face.

The pitch shot

A pitch shot is commonly used around the green, chiefly you need to drop the ball almost dead at your target. With this shot it is very easy to create backspin, allowing you to attack the flag if the green conditions allow. However, you could actually use this shot to approach a green from as far as 100 yards out. Its essential component is the backspin.

Playing the shot

Action		Effect
Position the ball slightly back in stance.	▶	Creates a downward blow from the golf club.
Open the face of the club slightly.	▶	Increases the loft of club for higher ball flight.
Open the stance, pointing the left foot slightly left of the target.	▶	Allows you to commit to the swing with acceleration.
Keep the stance narrow.	▶	Permits better shoulder rotation.

Backspin

Backspin is created by the speed of the club head and the angle of attack into the ball. You can increase the spin on the ball by speeding up the movement of the wrists within the swing.

Don't open the club face too much as it is important the ball travels the distance to the target.

The more loft you have the less distance gained, and this fact means that you can play this shot, with different clubs over a variety of distances.

The components that distinguish this shot from the chip are the increased spin and higher flight allowing the ball to stop dead on the green.

Ball motion when creating backspin. Controlled backspin on holding greens allows for greater accuracy of shot. It's easier to estimate and play for backspin than it is for release and roll. But you must know the nature of the greens on the day of play.

Divot or no divot

Taking a divot is an integral part of hitting a successful pitch shot, as is hitting the ball and turf in the correct order. A "ball to turf" contact is essential to generate backspin and ensure the required distance is achieved. Hitting the turf first results in a heavy or "fat" shot, leaving the ball woefully short and the golfer frustrated! The problem is that the ball is being hit too far up the club face, on a part of the club which does not propel the ball forward with any great speed. The correct strike is achieved through the hands and arms hitting down and through at impact. The body weight distribution should favor the left side slightly. Crucially, the club should not overtake the arms as you strike the ball. Commitment is everything here. Accelerate the club head through the ball with confidence for a great result.

Save a shot

Remember that the flag is rarely the target. Check your actual target before you play—try to ignore the flag at this point.

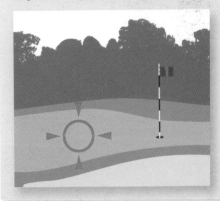

The chip shot

A chip shot is used around the green, ideally when you feel the need to drop the ball short of your target for it to run the rest of the way. What makes this different from the pitch shot is the lower ball flight and the reduction of spin on the ball.

Playing the shot

Action		Effect
Position the ball slightly back in stance.	▶	Creates a downward blow from the golf club.
Lean weight into the left side.	▶	Produces a downward blow.
Set the hands slightly ahead of the ball.	▶	Reduces the loft of the club for lower flight.
Grip the club as you would normally.	▶	Allows more control of wrist movement.
Choke down the golf grip.	▶	Increases your ability to control the golf club.
Keep the stance narrow.	▶	Permits better shoulder rotation.

Wrist movement

The reduction in spin is created by the lower speed of the club head and the different angle of attack into the ball. You can curtail the spin on the ball by reducing the movement of the wrists within the swing. You should feel as if you are sweeping the ball away with your club. Try not to open the face of the club as this will increase the height of the ball, preventing it from running out.

Clearly, the more loft you have the less distance gained. Since you are not really looking for loft you can play this shot with a variety of clubs over a range of distances. You could actually use this shot to approach a green from as far as 150 yards out.

It's worth noting also that if you reduce the spin on the ball then, when playing into wind, the ball will fly with less disruption.

When to play the shot

There are some general rules as to when this shot should be played (and, importantly, not played,) but generally you have to be dictated to by the situation, the course, and how well or confident you are in that shot on the day. The photos opposite set out the principles.

Remember, however, that the reduced ball spin and lower ball flight allows the ball to run on. For this reason the chip shot is favorite when you feel unable to create backspin or stop the ball. This will normally be when the green is firm or you are playing downhill or down wind. The key to a chip shot and achieving the correct angle of attack is to resist the temptation to try and help the ball in the air.

Pitch or chip?

Many young golfers watch television and see the incredible ability of the world's best golfers to generate backspin. This is popularly known as target golf and, although it's great to hit the ball hole-high with backspin, you are probably more likely to hole a chip shot by hitting the ground and letting the ball roll.

The chip shot is safer in many situations around the green, although not as effective when faced with carry-over hazards such as a bunker. You also have to make a more difficult choice when faced with a heavily contoured green. In these situations you have to be able to read the terrain well for a chip to roll out successfully. A high pitch here would take the contours out of the equation.

If faced with a situation where there is no right answer add one more element into the process—the shot you hit better on the day. Make your choice and then hit with conviction.

Save a shot

Because you are used to committing to full swing shots, especially on the tee, don't do anything less with your shots around the green. The most common and damaging fault is to decelerate the club head, hitting the ball fat.

The bump and run

The bump and run shot is similar in some ways to the chip shot. The key difference between the two shot types is the amount of time the ball spends in the air. The bump and run is what it says: a "bump" into play and a "run" up to the hole.

The bump and run can be played from any distance, normally up to about 40–50 yards from the green. Once the ball hits the green it has every opportunity to run into the hole if you find the correct line just as you would when putting. The bump and run will traditionally require an 8 iron up and can go up as far as a 3 wood. The backswing should be equaled in length by the through swing. The hands should be light with firm wrists and the timing of the swing should be even from start to finish. Close to the green the shot is pared down even more to become what we can call a chip-putt.

Playing the shot

Action		Effect
Position the ball in the middle of the stance.	▶	Constancy of strike.
Stand with your weight 60–40 to your left side (into the strike.	▶	Downward blow.
Grip the club as normal but choke down the shaft.	▶	Allows greater directional control.
Firm wrists	▶	Reduces danger of "floppy" or fat shot.
Keep your feet about hip width apart.	▶	Reduces excess body movement.

Hitting the chip-putt

Traditionally the shot is played with a regular set-up with a 7-, 8-, or 9-iron. The set-up is as for a regular putter but the stroke is more like a bump and run. The shot is not just a blend of two other shots but a stroke in its own right.

One way of approaching the bump and run shot is to stand over the ball more with the heel of the club in the air; the ball is addressed out of the toe. It looks ugly but it does offer you more of a putting set-up but with a longer club. In the stroke you will get a dead feel but this allows you to hit the ball harder, but with more control. The important thing here is to have only have the toe touching the ground. This reduces the drag you can get from the grass.

Striking the ball off the toe of the club.

A putter or an iron?

The putter can be successful when making a bump and run or chip-putt shot. It offers the percentage shot, almost guaranteeing a putting opportunity next. Judging the pace of the fringe grass and then the green can be tricky, particularly on fast greens offering contrast.

If the club selection is an iron, which one? Options range from wedge to 7-iron. The key is the distance the ball needs to fly before starting its run.

Save a shot

If your ball is going to run on the ground before it reaches the green (most noticeably with a bump and run shot) then take as much care with reading this ground as with the green. Is the grass long, wet, short, dry etc.?

The lob shot

This is perhaps the hardest shot to play. Its purpose is to carry the ball over hazards and to stop the ball dead after it's flight. In many ways the lob is simply an advanced pitch shot—where everything you do is exaggerated. Crucially this shot requires commitment and confidence and should be used only when you have no other choice but to pop the ball up in the air and get it straight back down quickly.

Playing the shot

Action		Effect
Position the ball in the middle of the stance.	➤	Promotes consistency of strike.
Open the face of the club even more than for the pitch shot.	➤	Increases the loft of club for higher ball flight.
Open the stance left of the target.	➤	Allows commitment to the swing with acceleration.
Keep your feet slightly wider apart than for pitch.	➤	Provides a stable base because the swing is longer and faster than the pitch.

You will be in trouble if you pop the ball up too much, hit it fat or scoop it, or decelerate the club. Play the lob shot well and you have turned a potentially bad situation into a very good one—and boosted your confidence in the process.

What wedges do you need?

A typical golf set contains two wedges: pitching wedge and sand wedge.

As players improve, they should consider adding wedges to their bag enabling them to broaden their repertoire of shots. Technology has moved on with wedges. Clubs offering every conceivable loft can be purchased including the lob and gap wedges. The lob wedge, typically with a 58 or 60-degree loft, offers extreme elevation with minimum roll. The gap wedge, with a loft of between 50–54 degrees, fills the gap between a pitching (45–48 degrees) and a sand wedge (55–59 degrees).

Wedges have been designed to accommodate the modern game of golf so it is important to find a set of wedges that suits your game and allows you to play the short game shots. To do this, borrow some demo clubs and practise hard at this area of the game. Wedges can allow you to escape difficult situations as well as to capitalize on good chances.

It does not help if you buy a full set of irons with matching wedges. Often these are not blade-like clubs but instead very large-headed clubs.

Swing speed and control

To play the shot you open the face up even more than for the pitch shot and come down sharply on the ball. Unlike the pitch shot, you are aiming for slightly increased acceleration in the club head as it strikes the ball. A clean strike will send the ball at a very steep angle. Anything less than clean will be a problem. The big danger in increasing the club head speed is thinning the ball.

The difficulty here is marrying-up increased speed with control. There is no easy answer to this. It's a necessary balance in a number of shots and can be achieved only with good practice. And with good practice comes confidence. There are many similarities between the lob and the "explosion" shot from the bunker, so if you can play one you can probably play the other.

Some golfers will never attempt this kind of shot in a round but, for genuine improvement, you need to have every shot in your repertoire.

Save a shot

Check the lie of your ball before making a shot selection. A tight lie might mean a bump and run shot is better than a pitch or a lob shot. Can you get a blade behind the ball or is there a danger of it bouncing off hard ground and thinning the shot? Is the grass long, wet, short, dry etc.?

Executing your shots

Once you feel comfortable with your choice of short-game shot, you then have to decide how you are going to play the ball.

Loren Roberts pitching to the green from light, fluffy rough. The hands are well forward at the very open club face allowing the ball to fly off the club at a steep angle. This should mean the ball comes to rest very close to where it pitches.

> **Save a shot**
> From club selection to celebration the short game requires strong mental discipline. Be extra vigilant near the green, and don't be disappointed because you made a poor decision or poorly executed shot.

Observation

When reading the green you are looking for the point where you are going to land the ball. This will be determined by:

- the shot you have chosen
- the line on which the ball will roll to the hole
- the pace of the green.

Try to develop a mental picture of how you want the ball to react. Then you will be able to calculate where the ball needs to land. If you are playing well and can put the ball approximately where you want to—and most top players can, of course, do this—then the observation phase of the game becomes more important. If you choose a target, then hit it; if the ball doesn't get close to the hole you have a problem with reading, not shot making.

Feel

To develop "feel" for a shot it is important to first have a consistent, rhythmical, and natural stroke. This comes from pre-round practice and earlier practice sessions. Good practice creates great understanding. You need to be able to trust your own abilities to make your shot.

Set-up

Your set-up should see you address the ball in a relaxed manner which allows you to aim straight at your target point i.e. the place in which you wish the ball to land, not usually the flag. Remember all your fundamentals and if you change your mind over a shot, perhaps switching from pitch to chip, change your set-up. To try to play one shot with the set-up for another is a common fault.

Focus

The very last thought with your short game should be the point on the ground where you wish to land the ball. This should be the only thought in your head as you play the shot. A good exercise is to find, and focus, upon a distinctive shadow or a slightly different shade of grass. This target should be established before your set-up and then, once ready to play, you should have one last glance at that target and then let everything else just happen.

Celebration

Celebration should also play a large part in your short game. Use celebration as a way of increasing positive emotional effect for the future. Tiger Woods was noted for his emotional explosion on the 16th hole at Augusta National in the 2005 Masters where he holed an impossible chip which assisted him with a wonderful win that year. He has had the benefit of seeing that replay on television time and time again.

But without television would he still have the same positive emotion when he visualizes that same shot? Yes, without question, because he marked that point in time with a strong response, a major celebration.

The concept of celebration is linked with reinforced responses. If, every time you do something bad you are told about it then your fear and anxiety create a situation in which you are likely to repeat the bad event. Conversely, if you celebrate a good shot, you are going some way to creating a positive ambience in which you are more likely to repeat the positive action. Choose a celebration (this will come naturally of course) that reflects your character and pleasure and don't be shy in demonstrating it. In essence, try with every great moment in your game to reinforce the memory with an emotion. This will give that great moment longevity.

The swing

Can you find the perfect swing? No. The "perfect swing" is a myth. All you can look for is the best possible result from each and every shot that you make. You can probably improve your game by changing your goals, not losing yourself in the search for perfection which even the greatest players haven't found.

Myth of the swing

Can anyone shoot 54 on a golf course (the equivalent of 18
birdies on a par 72)? Most good players have had a birdie on every
golf hole at their home course but none has been able to achieve this
result all in one game apart from maybe on a computer game. So will
this score ever be achieved? Yes it could, if you believe enough. A
good swing is not the only secret for success—but it is a very important
starting point.

The "look" of the swing

If you knew you were going to shoot your best
ever score today, would it matter how your
swing looked? No. It is the result that is
important. There is a tendency to stand over
the ball and concentrate too much on the
swing plane or the takeaway position, or on
weight transference during your swing, when
your real focus should be on what you are
trying to achieve.

Your aim is to hit the ball to your chosen
destination, and to do so you need to find a
shot that works. Then practice that to create

repeatability and a knowledge of what works
and what does not work. In this instance,
practice can't make perfect but it can help a
great deal.

What are you looking for?

This drill is to help you learn to turn on, as well
as turn off, on the course. The "play line" in
question is an imaginary point of no return. All
golfers actually use this drill with every shot
they play when on the course... we just don't
use it well.

Repeatability

Repetition breeds confidence, the confidence to
address the ball when full of positive thoughts. A
14 handicap golfer will make around 50 swings
from tee or fairway in an average round; this
means 50 opportunities to reinforce an effective
swing under match conditions. Time on the practice
ground is important too. Practice makes
permanent. Always try to practice with purpose.

But what type of swing should you practice?
One that suits you, feels comfortable, and achieves

the right result. Some players swing the club more
around their bodies, some use the hands and arms
to generate club head speed, and others use a
greater body turn. Physique will have an influence.
If you are short, swing more around or flatter.

If you are tall you will probably swing more
upright. A swing which "feels right" will be more
repeatable. More repeatable means more
consistent. More consistent means lower scores.

The play line can be called the commitment line—once crossed there is no return. If you imagine a line between you and the ball then, once the line has been crossed, you must move that ball on. What you need to do before you cross the line is plan *where* you want to move the ball to and *how* you will get it there. Once you have made a firm decision and are committed to that in your head you are ready to cross the play line. Once the line has been crossed, the only thing you should have in your head is the target that you are aiming for. You will be free of technical information, "what ifs," doubts. You can focus on the target and let everything else be natural and instinctive (See page 93).

The ball's flight, as evidence, is crucial in building a swing that suits you. When you are happy with the "evidence" then you can be happy with the swing. Build on this and start the process of creating repeatability—using the same effective swing every time.

The South African Ernie Els has one of the most envied swings in the modern game. He is a tall man, which helps but is not essential. He generates his considerable power with great acceleration into impact, aided by wrist movement.

The grip

Although there is no such thing as the perfect swing, there certainly are key basics that help build up an effective and efficient shot. One of these is the grip—the way you hold the club. The purpose of the grip is to hold the tool correctly and to allow that tool to perform to the best of its ability.

This should be done with the least amount of grip pressure from the hands. The tenser the grip the less freedom the club has to move freely into the ball. In the short term tension can offer control... but less feel and distance.

Although you will have chosen a grip when you started lessons it is always worth going back to this fundamental part of your game. Constantly check your grip, and be aware of why you grip the club as you do.

Choose your grip

The three main grips are shown right. With these grips the club should sit between the fingers and the fleshy part of the palm, offering the golf club a secure and stable point in order for the body to work the club.

The overlapping and interlocking grips are very close in hand positioning, apart from the point where the two grips meet. The baseball grip is the least common grip of the three and means the hands cover more of the club's handle grip but the principle is the same, the V that is formed by your right hand should lie parallel to the V on your left hand.

The interlocking (middle) and Vardon (bottom) grips allow the hands to work together. The baseball grip (top) can generate good power but there is a danger of one hand, the right, becoming dominant.

Weak and strong grips

The V that is between the thumb and forefinger should point between your right shoulder and the centre of your chin. If you have this V pointing at your right shoulder then you have a strong grip.

For good players this type of position may cause you to hook the ball and may mean you have to weaken the position by getting the grip to point closer to that of your chin.

The correct grip is the one that allows you to deliver the club head square to the ball at impact. The stronger grip may get too strong with time but only requires a slight adjustment as shown below. You will know when it is time for this by the hooking ball flight you will repeat.

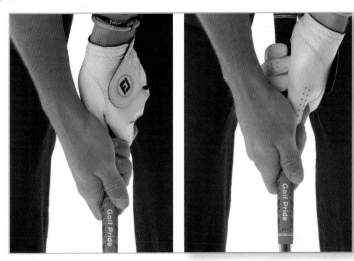

Weak (left) and strong grips. Watch you don't fall into one or the other as you try to correct other errors.

Applying the grip

Applying the grip can be done in four easy steps. Steps that are fundamental to the swing.

- Try always to feel that you have fall control of the club. This can only be done with a full grasp of the club. Never hold the club too close to the end of the grip.
- When placing the club into your left hand the grip should sit diagonally across the middle joint on your forefinger, continuing down to the base of the little finger. The best indication of this is when you can hold the club in-between your first three fingers and the fleshy part of your hand. When closing your hand to sustain this grip position you will form a V between your

forefinger and thumb, giving you the indication of grip strength.

- Now add the right hand without interfering with your already set left hand. How the right is applied will differ from one golfer to the next, depending on which grip they find most comfortable.
- Your grip pressure is the next key element. There is no hard and fast rule to this but your grip pressure should be light. From a scale of 1–10, ten being as hard as you can grip the club, your pressure should be around four, which is enough to hold the club but still allow freedom of movement without tension.

Alignment

How you address the ball with the club is a reflection of how you want to strike the ball at the point of impact. Clearly the grip can directly affect the position of the club face at address. These two elements (grip and lie) should work together, in harmony, so that everything feels natural.

When you take hold of any club ensure the head sits square to the target and ensure you are able to return that club to the square position at impact. By having the toe of the club sticking up too much you may turn the club head over, sending the ball on a inside line of the target. If the toe is too far down you may feel the grip trying to turn in your hands, causing a push or cut.

Check the lie angles of all your clubs. You can learn alignment quickly and easily, building upon the core basics to a situation that suits you. It's equally easy to let good practice slip, to fall out of alignment. At first your body will make adjustments and you may not notice too much wrong but eventually you'll be hitting bad shots and won't know why. Check—and continually re-check—your alignment. This normally requires a third eye.

Alignment comprises five key elements that all need to be square to the intended line of the ball:
- *shoulders*
- *hips*
- *knees*
- *feet*
- *club head.*

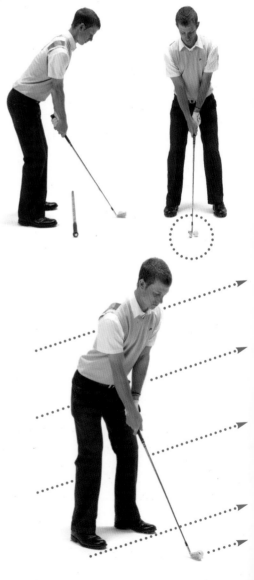

Routine

Getting yourself properly aligned is not too hard… but you need to build the process into a routine that works every time.

- Grip the golf club properly whilst taking aim at your target. Mentally construct a line back from your target to the ball. Then break this down by finding a nearer point to focus on when standing over the ball. Make sure, as you set the club head down, you have it square to the point of focus.
- Once you have the club head in the right position your right foot should sit parallel to the club head.
- Now bring in your left foot alongside your right and try to square this up with the imaginary line that can be drawn between the club head and the focus point.
- This should now allow you to align your shoulders with your feet. Ensure you do not adjust the square club face as you do this.

There is a danger of concentrating solely on alignment to the target and not with the ball. Also error might creep in if you have second thoughts on the tee and alter just one part of the set-up.

Perfect parallel alignment

Achieving this involves the feet, hips, and shoulders being square to the club face position. This orthodox set-up will improve the quality of the whole swing and enable you to hit straight shots, consistently. The use of imagery may help here; think railway lines. Imagine the club head, ball, and target on one rail and the feet, hips, knees, and shoulders on the other.

Watch how much trouble the pros take over their set-up before striking the ball. They realize that mistakes made at set-up result in loss of distance or inaccuracy. Often golfers believe they have achieved parallel alignment when in fact they have taken up either a closed or open stance which may result in an unwanted ball movement, left or right.

When practising, use additional clubs to check the alignment in order to develop good habits to take onto the course.

Stance and posture

A good stance is essential, especially as it gives you the base from which to swing. The swing plane can often force the body to overextend with excessive movement. By developing a good stance you are able to ensure balance. Balance will offer a good stable platform to generate the power you need to strike the ball with control.

The stance

The stance needed to create the stable foundation and good rotation comes from your feet and legs. By having your legs too close you lose the ability to stabilize the body during the swing rotation. Equally, having the feet too far apart will reduce the ability to rotate. You need to find the most stable stance which is normally when your feet are about shoulder width apart. This will allow you, in the swing, to load that right side in a stable manner.

Some teachers will say that you need to have your feet further apart the higher up the clubs you go, closer together for the high number irons and wedges. There is sense in this recommendation as you need the most stable base for the longest club/swing. But it is not essential. Remember that your clubs were probably measured for a standard, shoulder-width stance. If you have your feet too close together you may be standing too tall for a good posture.

Your width of stance is a source of power, created when transferring your weight from you rear leg to your leading leg on the downswing.

The posture

The posture should be natural allowing the body to feel comfort at address. You do not want to feel as if you are trying either to sit down or to fall forward. Remember how important balance is to the stability of the swing. It is something you need to try for yourself until you are happy, but think in terms of the following.

- With your feet and legs in a good position you should have a gentle flex in the knees, providing the feeling of being grounded at the base.
- Your knee flex should counter the tilt at the hips which arcs your back forward allowing the shoulders to sit directly over your toes.
- Your shoulders should have a good clearing from the chin so as to allow the shoulders to swing freely without interference from the chin. If the chin is moved by the shoulders the head will follow, and this will cause you to sway in the backswing.
- Your arms should have a small extension away from the body; this should be natural to the wrist extension, allowing you to put the club almost flat on the ground.

It is important to keep the back comfortable and straight for the best development of technique and constancy.

The dangers in an incorrect set-up are numerous. If you find you are sitting too far back from the ball (left), perhaps in an effort to get a wider swing, you will start to put the weight on your heels. The reverse is true if you lean too far over the ball, perhaps when getting anxious and trying to "steer" a shot, when the weight will be on your toes. Both errors will make you lose stability and may also result in hooks or cuts.

Visualization

Visualization is an important part of your routine, a mental skill which brings mind and body together. If it is to become embedded, visualisation must be practised. Before taking up the address position, picture the type of shot you would like to play. Imagine the ball flying through the air with fade or draw and see it landing in the target area and rolling to the intended destination. Stand directly behind the ball to do this job. Visualization focuses the mind on the shot, creating tunnel vision and helping to block out unwanted distractions. As you improve, your mental library of successful shots will expand. Although the execution may not be perfect, visualization helps build a positive mental picture which in turn builds confidence. Although a positive approach is essential it should be realistic also. If the shot is particularly tough, do not imagine a miracle shot.

Weight transfer

Loading is the transfer of weight to the right side (for right-handed golfers) by rotating the hips and shoulders. The transfer of weight is not a sway onto the right side. This is a misinterpretation made by many golfers following a swing lesson. It is a simple rotation of about 45 degrees of the hips that loads your right side.

If the hip rotation is simple and steady then the shoulders are also able to move in a concurrent manner, both utilizing a stable base. The shoulder rotation should be pushing 90 degrees. By applying the correct rotation to your right leg you will allow the body to "recoil," generating a down swing with the full body weight behind it.

Your rotation and weight transference are intrinsically linked with the all-important takeaway. This is the movement of the golf club away from the address position. There are two key thoughts as you begin the takeaway:
- the swing should be free moving not mechanical
- there should be a good transition at the top of the swing.

The weight transference and head movement are near perfect in this sequence. Watch good players and instructional DVDs for information and also record your own swing.

With these two thoughts in mind, think about the takeaway.

At half way the club shaft should be presenting itself squarely to your feet... which should be aligned to the intended target line.

This is a neutral takeaway position. Anything away from this line will be "outside" or "inside" the neutral takeaway line. A neutral takeaway is vital in creating, throughout the whole swing, a good swing plane.

*The neutral takeaway (left) is ideal. Your own swing may be outside this line causing your swing plane (right) to be too flat (**A**) or upright (**B**). You can still produce acceptable shots but for accuracy and, crucially, repeatability, aim for a neutral takeaway and a neutral swing plane.*

Weight transfer—throughout the swing

Effective weight transfer is equally important on the downswing, through impact, and into the follow-through. The shift of weight back toward the target starts before the club begins its downward path. This helps a correct swing path to the ball and also avoids an "arms only" swing.

Crucially, power is generated at impact by this movement. With the swing finished, weight transfer from the right side to the left side is complete with the right toe left merely as support.

Practice drills can help. Take a 5 iron and stand with your feet firmly on the ground as though stuck with glue.

Hit some shots and feel the lack of weight transfer particularly at impact. Poor shots will flow! Then start working on a smooth transfer: weight onto the right side during the backswing, back to the left on the downswing. Feel the difference in the quality of the strike and the power generated.

Swing plane

The swing plane is the path that the golf club takes to the top of the swing and then back to the ball and through. The swing plane is largely dictated by the takeaway position. From a neutral takeaway position your swing plane should also be neutral, or "straight up" and "straight down." If this can be achieved, there is a greater chance of ensuring that the club face is square at impact, essential for consistent striking.

Sean O'Hair demonstrating an excellent swing plane playing in the PODS Championship at Palm Harbor, Florida. At the top of this neutral swing his back is fully turned and the club's toe is pointing to the target.

Self-correction

Many players are able to self-correct an incorrect takeaway. Somewhere through the transition phase at the top of the swing there is a movement which corrects this initial error. However, clearly, the swing plane is far more efficient when the club swings along the neutral line. This provides the consistency needed to create a repeatable ball strike. You don't want to build in too many compensations for errors in your swing.

Players who self-correct the golf club when it is moving outside their swing plane line are said to be casting the club, and are changing their angle of attack into the ball. In this instance the club head will be cutting across the ball starting the attack from the outside of the ball. This will cause the ball to start its flight left of your target. This can also result in you causing a fade. The opposite is also true when your downswing compensation returns on the inside of the line. The effect this has will start the ball outside your target line and will sometimes cause a draw flight.

Checking your swing plane

Swing a 5 iron holding the club at the top of the backswing. Hands should be positioned above your right shoulder with your back ideally facing the target. This swing plane allows you to constantly strike the ball and deliver the club head back to the ball in a square position, creating a well hit straighter shot. A swing plane

that is too steep will produce a heavier strike which will start left of target producing a fade or slice. When the swing becomes too flat often a player will compensate by looping at the top of the back swing which could cause a number of ball flights and not allow any form of consistence for the player.

Consistency is the key and you can work on this by coming back to the basics shown in the diagram. The ball (as it lies or correctly teed) plus the club (carefully chosen) plus your thoughts (simple and clear) plus your physical readiness (your set-up) produce the swing. It's the same every time.

The components of your swing: the ball plus the club plus your thoughts/plans plus your physical readiness equals your swing. It's then the same every time.

Impact

The impact is the point where you actually strike the ball. If you can consistently strike the ball correctly, that is what matters. However, you are much more likely to hit the ball correctly if you adopt the classic grip, stance, posture, alignment and swing.

Impact and club head speed

For the correct position the club head should resemble how the club looked at the address position providing, of course, that you were set-up correctly and were square to the target.

To gain distance from the ball you need to generate club head speed. The faster the club head is travelling at impact the more distance can be gained by the ball. But be aware, club head speed does not just come from the hands but also from the shoulders, hips, and knees. They all generate more speed from each other.

Tiger at impact:
- *Head stays level or behind the ball.*
- *Shoulders are slightly open to target.*
- *Hips will lead the swing see how they are also open to target.*
- *Right knee is turning in towards the left knee which will bring the outside of the right foot and heel slightly off the ground placing 65% of the weight onto the left side.*
- *The shaft and left arm forming a straight line through impact.*

Connected swing

An overemphasis on use of hands and arms to generate club head speed results in the club face opening and closing too quickly. The player will be unable to visualize where the club face is at any point of the swing. The temptation to compensate for the club head being in the wrong position will be irresistible. **The result**: Inconsistent ball striking and poor shots. **The solution**: Good body rotation combined with effective transfer of weight from the right side to the left. This is the "engine" of your golf swing, producing club head speed at impact.

Power is created through body leverage and the involvement of large muscle groups—not by using just sheer effort with arms and hands. In a connected swing the club head moves in tune with your body with the club face opening and closing more slowly. With less to do and think about, a more repeatable, consistent swing is possible.

In every sport in which you have to hit an object with a club, racket, bat, or one of your limbs there is a through motion. A boxer, for example, is looking for a point past the impact stage. This is much the same in tennis or baseball. The greater the movement past the impact point implies greater intent. With a golf shot, you can learn to control the distance of clubs with feel and practice. The important factor is that a relaxed, but extended, through swing will provide greater ball distance.

If you have good fundamentals and are set-up square to the target, you then need to focus on how you want to finish. This thought will allow the subconscious to control your swing. By doing this you will tell your body where you want to go.

Thinking beyond the point of impact is a technique taught to boxers that can also help golfers.
The boxer and golfer are both aiming to hit through the point of impact to a target slightly beyond.

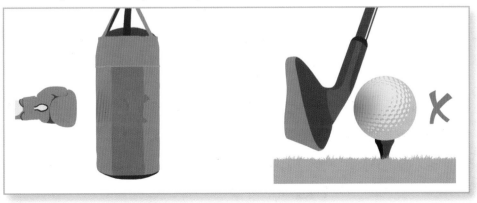

Shaping the shot

When shaping your shots you need to change your club to suit the shot and the distance. When you open the face of your club to produce a fade, you are increasing the loft on that club which will shorten the distance the golf ball carries. Closing the face of the club to help create a draw flight can cause you to deloft the club head face, resulting in lower ball flight and more distance.

Keep it simple

It is easy to complicate fade and draw shots or to adapt your own simple techniques to make do. A simple explanation of both shots confirms that they are relatively easy to produce. The time and effort that you expend will give you confidence to play and control both the fade and the draw.

When playing a draw you should have two main things in your mind: your target, and your target line. With a normal shot your target and target line are the same. With a draw your target does not change but your target line does. Set your target line to the right of your target. Once you have this in mind set your stance square to that target line and close the club head face onto your target. Your swing plane stays natural to your target line; it is the club head that will draw the ball back onto your target.

The opposite is true of the fade. The target line should now be left of your target, creating a new target line and the face should be open to this, which should see the club face facing your target. Again, keep the swing plan natural and allow the club face to produce the results.

With both shots the more you play the greater the understanding you will have on distance and how much you need to move the ball off the target line for it to come back in. Knowing how to shape the ball will help you identify issues when you hit the ball off line.

The set up for a fade, with the club head facing the target and the feet open to the target which indicates where the player will start the flight of the ball. The swing plane must follow the feet. If attempting a fade (right) or draw (left) keep your thinking clear. This is my swing plane, this is my target.

Playing naturally

If you can understand how club head positions and angles of attack alter ball flight then you can begin to play less consciously, more naturally. As you develop your game, and play and practise more, you will get to realize that different types of swing create different ball flights. Using fade and draw will become part of the improving golfer's armory to navigate their way around the course.

But be sure to know why you are intending to play a shaped shot. The way the ball reacts when it hits the ground will not suit all situations. Visualization is the key. You need to see the shot to feel it, imagining the ball bending in its flight to the target.

Top players such as Ian Poulter will be able to shape shots using feel and subtle hand movements.

Feel, set-up, execution

Swing, shot shape, feel... these are all part of the process. But possessing the knowledge and skill are not enough. As you improve you need to work beyond a basic understanding of the swing fundamentals; it is time to develop your feel for the shot. Feel develops from the relationship between your conscious and subconscious thoughts, before or during the swing.

You could look at the ball and say "I'll just make a swing and hit the ball over there." Hitting the ball with very little, or no, pre-shot preparation is not going to produce the result. You need a plan—you need a routine.

You can think of this process in the same way a chess player would plan each move that he makes. And you need to have a repeatable process that you can adopt on every shot.

Learning from others

All the great sportsmen and sportswomen in the world today have a routine which is carried out like a ritual. Often these routines have a mannerism that makes it personal to that

individual. Some players pace up and down. Tiger prowls! A tennis player may sway from side to side on the court line before receiving a serve, or as a basketball player, before a free throw, might bounce the ball three times before making the shot. In many cases the trigger mechanism also helps the physical process—keeping warmed up, on your toes, settled etc.

You should find a mannerism that you can put into your routine—something that is personal to you—this will act as a trigger to begin the process. See what you do naturally and build on this. Feel comfortable with the mannerism. Don't make it self-conscious in any way.

Serena Williams prepares to serve, holding the ball in the V of the racket head. Small recurring rituals help promote the all-important repeatability.

Your swing routine

Stage 1 Red

You need to assess the shot. This is the thinking zone. You should not have your bag on your shoulders or be talking to others in your group. Your thoughts before you make the commitment to address the ball should comprise:

- What is my target?
- How far do I have to my target?
- How does the ball sit?
- Will the wind affect the distance or movement of the ball?
- What club do I need to make this shot?

On your marks

Stage 2 Amber

Once you are clear about the information in Stage 1, the next stage is your final thoughts before you make the commitment to swing:

- How do I want the ball to land?
- How do I hit the ball to gain the best result?
- How should I set-up to the ball?
- Where is that target (again)?

Get ready

Stage 3 Green

- Now hit the ball!

Go

A good routine should allow you to play with a clear mind with no outside influences. This is difficult in golf because the ball is still. In other sports, like tennis, the player is reactive to the moving ball and the decision is a thousand times quicker.

Try, with any routine you use, to spend no more than 20 seconds making your decision and about three seconds stood over the ball. This will reduce the time you need to concentrate on the shot and should prevent you from getting mentally tired while playing.

Out of trouble

As you cannot avoid the hazards on the golf course, there is no point in worrying about them. What is key to your game is how you chose to manage these hazards. If you always go in search of glory you are likely to fail in the bold but blind pursuit for miracle shoots. What you can do, instead is have good techniques for playing tricky shots and a good brain for deciding when not to play a particular shot.

Out of the rough

The game would be very boring if you played a perfect round of golf, even though for enthusiastic golfers this is the aim. There will always be times on the course when you find yourself in an awkward situation. Try to accept these with equanimity and turn them into your chance to produce the best shot of the round. Most commonly a bad shot will put you in the rough.

When you start playing the game a shot out of the rough can put you into panic. As your game improves you need to take a more considered approach. It is not the end of your round; it may mean one extra shot but maybe not even that. Having decided what you hope to achieve, break down your thinking into separate, related, elements:

- what type of rough
- what club to use
- what shot to play.

What type of rough

Not all rough is the same. You have to think carefully about the nature of the stuff you are in. This is not highly technical. It is down to your experience and common sense. But, to play better golf, you have to think carefully. In the light rough you should look at the cut, or nap. Normally it will be orientated towards the hole, aiding you. But not always. You will get less distance and control against the nap. In deeper rough you need to assess the nature of the vegetation. Wet or dry, spindly or thick. Your own experience is the guide here. Have you played from this kind of stuff before? What was the result? You have to be realistic. Importantly what is behind, and in front of, your ball. Tall grass or weeds in front may impair the flight of the ball. Thick stuff behind the ball can turn the club in your hand or cause deceleration.

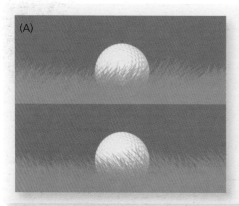

(A)

(B)

What club to use

When playing from the thick stuff the most common fault among amateur golfers is to play with too much club. Always assess your lie and be confident you have the right club for the job. The more loft the better in this type of situation.

You will almost certainly lose some control of the ball from the rough so your judgment of distance will be harder. Sometimes you will "get a flier" while other times distance will be impeded. Don't simply think longer or shorter but weigh up the dangers. Where is there more danger?

As mentioned above, it's normally better to use a higher angled iron to ensure that you get out of the rough rather than going for distance although, out of wispy or light rough you can often get a rescue club/hybrid at the ball. The extra weight behind the blade will help you push right through the shot.

What shot to play

Again, simple rules cannot be applied universally; you have to assess the situation and use your experience and judgment. In general you can think about three issues.

When attempting to get out of deep stuff, use a **steep angle** in the back swing so you are chopping down slightly on the ball. The more dense the rough and the more imperative it is "just to get out," the steeper the angle.

Although a loose grip is recommended for most golf shots the rough demands a **firmer grip** (not "stronger"). This is to prevent the club from twisting either before or after the ball. Even with the chop down shot described above, try to grip firmer all through the shot.

Finally think carefully about an **accurate ball strike**. On the fairway you have a little bit of forgiveness provided by the surface and the bounce of the club. You may hit the ball fat or thin but the result may not be too bad. In the rough the ball may be resting on grass, away from a firm surface. You need to pick the ball off and not hit underneath it.

Watch out for the direction of the cut (A), the positioning of thicker vegetation (B) and the type of rough in which your ball lies (C).

Aim for the back of the ball and not the surface of the ground. Hitting underneath the ball may mean you flop it forward just a few feet.

(c)

Trees and obstacles

Improvization skills and good imagination are the greatest assets you can bring to a golf course when coping with trees, and other obstacles, that might obstruct your game. Think about the possible shots and possible outcomes in a realistic way before considering creative ways of getting back on track. Never forget that declaring a ball unplayable and taking a penalty drop is an option. If you really can't make a shot—don't try.

Assuming you are not dropping you may have four options:
- a cut around the tree
- a hook around the tree
- a shot over the tree
- a shot underneath the tree.

Frequently, of course, you only have one option.

With all shots, imagine the line along which you need to hit the ball for it to reach your target. Exaggerate all thoughts and movements. It is important to ensure you are clearing the hazard and the ball is getting back into play.

Cut shot

Because a cut shot will reduce the distance your ball will travel, you need to use a club or two more to replace that lost amount. To play this shot you will need to set your feet left of target in the direction you wish to start the ball, always keep the club face pointing at the target, that is where you want the ball to finish. Make sure you aim with your feet wide enough to get around the obstacle. To change the height of the ball, move it a fraction back in your stance for a lower flight.

Hook shot

The hook shot will, as a general rule, come out lower than a cut shot, so you should adjust your stance around the ball to change the height of the ball flight. To play this shot you will need to set your feet right of target again in the direction you wish to start the ball. Always keep the club face pointing at the target or where you want the ball to finish. Make sure you aim with your feet wide enough to get around the obstacle. You should always maintain a low shallow swing plane when hitting this shot. With both the cut and hook make sure to swing the club on the line of your feet and let the club head do the rest.

Under trees

In some situations you will want to hit underneath overhanging branches or foliage. Set the ball slightly back in your stance, placing your hands marginally forward—but take care not to overdo this. Transfer more of your weight to your leading side. Allow your rear leg to bend inward. This should give you the feeling of an impact position. Maintain this weight on your lead side in the backswing, and move from the shoulders not from your hands. Consider a less-lofted club in these situations.

The reverse shot

On occasion you will find it is impossible to swing the club in the traditional sense, playing right-handed or left-handed as you do. But through improvisation you can get around this problem by playing a reverse shot in order to avoid taking that dreaded drop. The reverse shot means you still play the ball with the front of the club's blade; this is not playing wrong-handed.

Over trees

There are occasions when you need to play over obstacles such as trees to reach your target. Try to be realistic when assessing this shot. Your golf club can offer some assistance here, but it is only a guide. If you are trying to measure what club will give you the height needed to carry the ball over the obstacle,

align the club with your ball. Then stand on the face of the club; the angle of the shaft will indicate the rough flight of your ball. To add to this ball height, set your ball slightly forward in your stance so the club will impact with the ball on the upswing.

Importantly thereafter, play your normal swing. Rushing or trying to force the height will result in a bad ball strike.

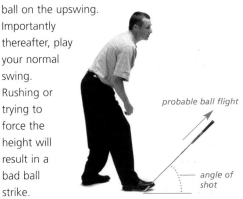

probable ball flight

angle of shot

This is only a rough guide but it is a starting point in your decision making.

Special shots

A The **wrong-handed shot**. Playing the opposite way to normal means using the back of the club or putter.

B The **backwards shot** played one-handed, often with a short iron. This is for short distance only and the ideal technique is to go down the shaft.

C The **reverse shot**. You can get good direction and distance with this shot if you practise effectively. It is a useful tool to have at your disposal.

In all three cases there is a great tendency to raise the head too quickly to see if you have been successful. Keep your head down and play rhythmically.

Shots off slopes

Most golfers do very little practising on sloping lies. Work on the range is nearly always off the flat. But playing challenging courses means having to deal with undulations in the ground. This contouring of the fairway can present you with a mixture of lies from ball above or below your feet to an uphill or downhill lie.

It is important to understand how these will affect your ball, and what you need to do to achieve the best possible results. The ball will naturally have a tendency to fly in the direction of the slope.

Balance is the key

With any sloping lie balance is the fundamental key to the shot you may face. Think about balance and remember the fundamentals as explained below.

Uphill lie

Because you are hitting the ball uphill choose an extra club to make up for the distance you will lose because of the increase in elevation. Then:

● align yourself right of your target to counter the slope

● set your weight onto your right side (this will allow the shoulders to be perpendicular to the slope)

● maintain balance throughout the swing

● follow though to a nice full finish.

Downhill lie

Because you are hitting the ball downhill, choose to club down to reduce distance of the ball. Then:

● align yourself left of your target to counter the slope

● set your weight onto your left side (this will allow the shoulders to be perpendicular to the slope)

● maintain balance throughout the swing

● follow though to a nice full finish.

You should try to align your shoulders with the slope to enable you to move through the ball more naturally at impact. If your shoulders are parallel to "level" ground you will have a tendency to swing out of sequence with the shoulders taking over.

uphill lie   *downhill lie*

Ball above feet

- grip down the shaft to reduce the length of the club
- aim right of the target accordingly to counter the reaction off the slope
- keep good balance at address
- ball slightly back of normal
- maintain balance during the swing
- keep the swing nice and smooth throughout.

Ball below feet

- hold the club at its fullest length to get the most out of the club and keep your balance
- aim left of the target accordingly to counter the reaction off the slope
- keep good balance at address
- ball normal according to the club
- maintain balance during the swing
- keep the swing nice and smooth throughout.

ball above the feet   *ball below the feet*

The hips should be used to make a comfortable and natural alignment meaning the weight is evenly balanced. You are trying, as far as possible, to give yourself a similar set-up to the one when you are standing on flat ground.

Playing with more touch

Think about the following and try to build these ideas into your natural, improving, game.

Ball above the feet

The easiest lie on a slope is when the ball is above your feet. This shot does not make you overstretch for the ball nor does it restrict your movement in the swing, but it can affect the club head. You must first know what is going to happen. If you lie the head of the club flat on the ground you will notice that the loft on the club face will be facing left of your target. Therefore it is easy to hook or push the ball from this position, and you may flatten the swing to that of the contours on the ground. You need to aim right of your target to accommodate this. Try also to use your hands more; do not guide the shot with your shoulders.

Ball below the feet

You will often find the ball sitting below your feet at address. When playing the shot from below your feet, the ball will tend to start left and to cut back in. This may occur if you have opened your club head because it appears to sit better when on the ground. It may also be difficult to balance because in this position you are leaning down the slope and there is a tendency for your lead shoulder to open as a way of trying to balance the body to that of the ground (only when the slope is severe). Counter this by bending your knees more at address. This will reduce that feeling of falling forward onto your toes. It will also minimize the stretch needed to hit the ball as you are now positioned near it.

Poor conditions

The two main problems that can affect your confidence and your scores are wet and windy weather. The former will not offer you any help but you can turn it to your advantage if you adapt better than your opponents. The latter may be seen as both positive and negative; your job is to manage the effects.

In order to play better golf it is important that you can cope with windy conditions, wet grips, and other adverse circumstances as these skills are needed to develop your game. If you try to avoid situations that make the game harder, then you may as well remove all the hazards from the course to make golf easier. Weather conditions are as much part of the game as bunkers are to the course. There is a lot more to be gained from playing in difficult situations, because to achieve a target when faced with a task that is so much greater than the norm is to feel a greater sense of achievement.

Peter Tomasulo and his caddie wait on the second tee during the final round of the Nationwide Tour Players Cup held at Pete Dye Golf Club in Bridgeport, West Virginia. Keeping concentration can be as hard as playing the shot in such adverse conditions.

In the rain

Be prepared with the **right clothing**. Learn to play your swing well in whatever you are wearing so you don't have negative thoughts during the bad weather.

Try to **keep gloves and grips dry** as far as possible but don't get disconcerted if they do get wet. A light grip on the club, even with wet gloves, will probably suffice.

Minimize other distractions. If you wear glasses, think about contact lenses. If the rain is intermittent keep wet proofs on rather than keep changing in and out of them. And in warm weather don't worry too much about getting wet. Soon enough you will be back in the clubhouse and dry.

In the wind

Try to **estimate the wind strength** in terms of clubs i.e. a one-club wind, a two-club wind etc. This will only come through practice.

Constantly **check the wind direction**. Both the orientation of the course, and the direction of the wind, will change as you play. Don't make assumptions; keep checking.

Don't overestimate the effect of wind on your shots. A firm, straight shot will cut through the wind and probably only be affected as it slows at the end of its flight.

Use the wind if it is with you or against you. In the former you can float the ball with it; in the latter you can expect the ball to stop in its flight more abruptly, therefore making it easier to drop gently to your target.

Finally, **learn how to play a low ball** when you require distance into a strong wind. From the tee, put the ball slightly back in the stance and use a lower tee peg. If you have a choice of club, go for the lower angle: a 3 wood instead of a 5 wood, a 6 instead of a 7 iron.

A positive attitude

Whatever the weather, always keep your head held high. This will keep you alert and motivated. The universal sign for "I am not happy" is when you see someone walking down the street with their head lowered. Get that chin up and show the world, and your opponents, your positive attitude.

Focus on the shot in hand, taking all the conditions into account; let this be the essential challenge. Golf is a game played outdoors with all that entails. No two rounds are the same and no two courses alike. That's all part of the game.

Planning any tricky shot

When considering this miracle shot you need to be absolutely sure that you can make the shot needed. If the certainty is not there in your own mind, then weigh up the alternatives (see page 98). Calculate where the best position is for the ball to land and what will give you the best place from which to play your next shot. A shot from a difficult position should be assessed much more carefully than any other shot you play on the course.

You must work out:
- what needs to be done to move the ball out of the current situation
- what will happen if you do not pull the shot off fully
- whether you can use the rules to help you
- whether there is an easier way to play the shot.

Above all, ensure you get the ball back into play. If you do not, then you will add more shots to your total and probably retain a bad memory of the hole.

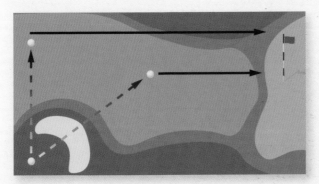

The safe shot may take you 150 yards from the green whereas the "ambitious" shot puts you 70 yards away. But if you can hit the green from both places, why take the risk?

Out of traps

To be in a sand trap is not an ideal location. However for veterans of the bunker game such a hazard can sometimes be the friendliest place around the green. You can gain considerable control when playing out of sand, as you are able to hit down through the ball into the sand with great speed.

With more speed you can add spin to the ball, which allows you to attack the pin position. Whenever in a trap always consider a more lofted club than your first thought.

Greenside bunker shots

Greenside bunkers generally have greater banks or lips than fairway ones, so you need to create a shot that can generate good height in a short distance—much like the lob shot. Assess your target, i.e. the flag position, as you would when playing any short-game shot, so the ball will land in the best possible position.

Move to the back of the bunker and then visualize the shot with a few practice swings. The greater the backswing the more distance will be gained.

Then get into the bunker, but be careful not to touch the sand with the club as this will incur a penalty. Allow the rear foot to sit at a right angle to the landing point on the green. Hover the club head open to your intended target. Then apply your lead foot to the sand in an open stance. You may need to adjust the width of the stance depending on the length of the shot and the contours inside the bunker.

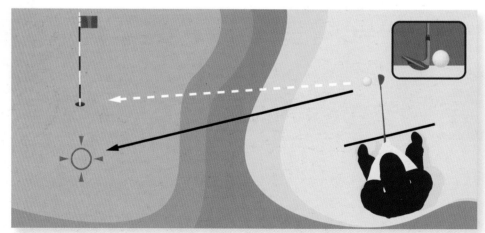

There are two angles to consider, that of your club face to the ball and also the angle of club to sand. Experiment but be confident in bunker play. The main problems can occur with deceleration through the ball so that too much sand is taken and the ball does not clear the front lip.

For a solid base to swing from, rotate your feet, shaking the loose sand from underneath them. Note when you do this how much sand there is in the bunker. This may serve as a guide as to how you tackle the shot. When applying the lead foot, make sure the club head does not close, i.e. hood the face. The shaft angle should move away from the target. This will keep the club face open, allowing you to use the sole of the club head more. With your feet aligned your shoulders will be open.

Check this, as this is the correct position and will create a more out-to-in swing, allowing you to cut under the ball and across the sand. This motion combined with soft hands will create a high flight and a soft landing.

The idea of this technique is to get the ball out of every bunker and this is best achieved when the ball is aligned on the leading foot. The bounce angle on the club will vary from one sand wedge to the next, as well as the types of bunkers you play. If you do struggle,

alter the openness of the club head to find what best suits the bunkers you play. Adjustments of the club face will also determine how *far* you hit the ball, providing there is acceleration from the club head through the ball.

Fairway bunker shots

Always consider what you might gain by hitting a long shot out of the sand as opposed to a lay-up shot. There may also be a lip to carry the ball over. It is essential to select the right club for the job, a club that primarily gets you out, secondarily gives you distance.

As a guide try to use a club or two more from a fairway bunker than from a greenside one, unless the ball is perched up. In this case beware of being too ambitious and taking sand with the shot. Any amount of sand will slow the club head down and so reduce distance. A gentle soft grip—just like the normal bunker shot—will increase club head speed and ball height.

The lie and the lip are the keys. Make sure you can pick the ball off without too much sand and ensure you have sufficient loft to clear the front of the bunker; do not be too greedy for distance.

Fit for Golf

Your general health and fitness are especially important if you are to play better golf. The information available on the components of fitness and how developing fitness can improve your performance is huge, and with the golfing market flooded with the latest training programs and "quick fix" gadgets it can be difficult to know where to start.

Back to basics

Understanding how your body works and moves is relevant if you want to improve your performance at golf. Once you have grasped this knowledge, you can analyse your own performance and develop a plan to improve weaker aspects of your fitness.

Designing training programs for golf is easier than most people think and relies simply on the "principles of training." By learning from the basic "proven" fundamentals, you can avoid potentially expensive personal trainers.

If until now your personal fitness has not been a priority for you, it is extremely important to gain an all-round functioning body before tackling golf-specific techniques. Only then can you really develop and get the most out of your game.

First steps

It is important to start in a methodical manner when developing your own fitness. Increasing your cardiovascular levels will ensure you have a suitable level of oxygen in the blood cells, allowing your body to perform better during training sessions and preventing injury. You must develop a suitable level of cardiovascular performance before committing to the development of your strength, flexibility, balance, muscular endurance, and speed.

*Named by **Men's Fitness** magazine as one of the fittest men in America—even when out with a serious injury— Tiger Woods has helped re-define the image of golf. Tiger's dedication to fitness is seen as an important part of his all-round game. He has helped to inspire countless other golfers to make all-round fitness a pre-requisite for playing the game.*

With this in mind it is always wise to seek advice from your doctor before committing to an increased level of exercise. Also control how much you commit initially to any increase in exercise.

Long-term benefits

Your fitness levels will very much dictate the amount of effort and application needed. This is not a reason to avoid fitness. It is essential to do these exercises as not only will they help you play the game you love but they will also reduce the risk of diseases, heart conditions, and other health-related problems. Steady exercise using the correct techniques will enable you to live much longer and so continue to play the game of golf more into your later years.

Although commitment to greater fitness will trigger an enhanced sense of well-being, when you actually start your training program you are unfortunately reminded about how unfit you are and how much of a struggle this fitness is going to be. Look past that; with good routine and struggling through those initial few weeks, you will find all the rewards you look for.

Components of fitness for golf

The four main areas that will help develop your performance are:
- aerobic endurance
- muscular fitness
- flexibility
- nutrition.

A combination of all these aspects is required to increase your fitness so you perform effectively in golf and any other physical activities.

Tip
Your warm up should be golf specific to mobilise the joints, increase flexibility and to prevent injury.

Aerobic endurance

Aerobic endurance is the body's ability to engage in sustained periods of physical exertion. Good aerobic endurance is the key component to the body's efficiency. Cardio-respiratory or aerobic efficiency is the ability of the heart to deliver oxygen in red blood cells to the required muscles as and when needed while transferring carbon dioxide from the muscles to the lungs, from where these noxious gases are expelled.

Sources of exercise

The types of exercise that will help you develop aerobic fitness include any repetitive movement that raises your heart rate such as:

- walking
- running
- swimming
- cycling
- rowing.

If, when doing any exercise like this, you do not achieve a reasonable increase in your heart rate, then you simply need to increase your work rate. This you will have to do in time anyway because of your heart's increased ability to deal with more exercise. The heart is a muscle much like any other in your body; the more you do the stronger it gets. However you must not exercise any harder than your heart will allow, and if you have any heart concerns always see your doctor before committing to any exercise regime.

Benefits

Aerobic endurance will allow your body to develop far quicker and more efficiently. It will provide greater stamina when playing a game of golf, reducing that tired body feeling toward the end of your round. It will also increase your levels of concentration during the round and in other aspects of your life.

Taking on aerobic exercise as part of your preparation for golf must be done in a considered and careful manner. Check with your physician if you have any concerns about your heart. A heart monitor will enable you to check how much you are increasing heart rate and whether you are within sensible limits.

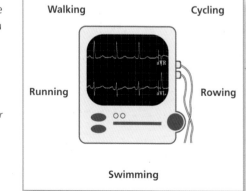

Walking   Cycling

Running   Rowing

Swimming

Hydration

Hydration is the source of fluid that maintains body temperature. The average daily intake of pure water should be $4^1/_2$–$5^1/_2$ US pints a day. When playing golf this could increase up to three times that amount. Your body requires this regular flow of fluid when exercising as it needs to sweat onto the skin before evaporating in order to keep you cool. If you sweat more than you are imbibing moisture, then your body will dehydrate, increasing your body temperature to dangerously high levels which can in some cases cause heat exhaustion. Such a scenario is not uncommon on the golf course.

Never wait until you are thirsty before drinking—always take regular, small amounts to stay hydrated. If you do find you are getting hotter than you should when playing golf, and you need to have some water at once, simply warm the water up and then drink it. This will pass through your system very quickly—a bit like putting water into a car that has overheated; when cold water hits a hot engine it reacts.

Although cold water is refreshing, your body will react and tense when digesting it. Any water that matches your body temperature will be absorbed quickly, for speedy hydration.

When it is cold, do not think that you require any less water. Your body in fact needs to use more energy than normal to stay warm, and this will also mean you will sweat more readily. Allow your body to be as efficient as it can with a good regular intake of water during the day.

Water and other liquids are important all year, not just in hot weather.

Tip

Go for a brisk one mile walk on the morning of a competition round. This will be great for aerobic fitness and should clear your mind ready for action!

Muscular fitness

The greater the number of repetitions when the muscle is applying force the greater the muscular endurance, which is the ability to maintain repeated contraction of the muscle or group of muscles. When playing golf you need muscular stamina to get round the course as well as when doing the endless drills in practice; this is mostly where muscular endurance plays its biggest role in the game.

Muscular endurance

At any endurance event there are two factors that make a golfer into an endurance golfer:

- repetition
- work time.

For example, when in training for a marathon or ultra marathon you have to repeat the running movement over and over—and so with golf when hitting balls. When you are going to overuse your muscles, there has to be a limit to these repetitions. You must therefore be smart when developing muscular endurance.

Never overdo one movement, otherwise you will increase injury risk. In order for your body to become accustomed to being put through its paces you should also complete other exercises that get you working for long periods of time. Create a structure to your training program by having a short focused session on, for example, running and then complementing this with work effort with other activities, swimming or cycling—to give you a more balanced regime.

In golf, focus one session on hitting controlled shots, making them count, and follow this by a break. Then start a new session in which you exercise other parts of your body and lightly work on the areas that you have already used to make your swing. In order to protect your body you should not go out and just hit endless balls on a driving range.

Muscular strength

This is the measure of how much force you can exert in a single movement. Muscular strength differs considerably from muscular endurance, which is the continuing ability to repeat the movement.

Everyone has two types of muscle fibres in their body: fast twitch and slow twitch muscle fibres.

The fast twitch muscle fibres are developed with exercises that gain you muscular strength—such as weightlifting or swinging a heavy golf club—and with any other exercise that requires a quick burst of energy. These are the muscle fibres that help a sprinter increase speed in a 100-metre sprint or a golfer deliver that controlled explosive swing that rockets the ball off the tee.

The slow twitch The slow twitch muscle fibres are those that use oxygen to generate "fuel" for continuous, long-lasting work. These fibres burn more slowly than fast twitch fibres and can go for a long time before they become exhausted. Therefore, slow twitch fibres are great at helping athletes run marathons and golfers stay alert and fresh over five-hour rounds.

Flexibility

Everyone needs to have a reasonable amount of motion to play golf. If this ability to move the body's joints is increased, then a large motion of movement is created, the arc of the swing is greater, and the swing becomes more powerful. Without this range of movement the stretching of tendons and joints will become tighter, reducing flexibility levels in your body.

Flexibility is the ability to move joints and muscles through their full range of motion; it is not the ability to move in a specific manner that suits the exercise. It plays a large part in physical fitness. Not all people have the same flexibility level but with sensible regular stretches this can be increased and maintained for great performance.

OK, you don't need to be this flexible but general body suppleness can only be an advantage in shaping your body to the game. This is Colombian Camilo Villegas lining up a putt; his posture allows him to view the line more perfectly than a player who has to turn his head sideways to view the line.

Tip

Next time you are watching the professionals, take note of their physique. Work out where they are strong, and use this knowledge to get going on some exercises in those areas yourself.

Nutrition

Although, to some people, golf may not look like a sport that requires a good level of fitness coupled with a sufficient quantity of nutritional food intake, they would be very wrong.

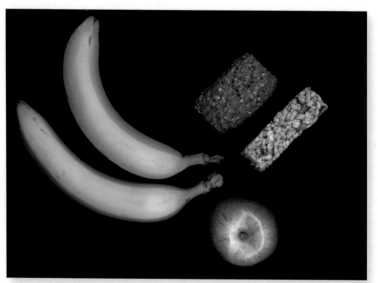

It is important to think about keeping the body's energy levels up when playing a round of golf. Get into the habit of taking a healthy snack out with you.

Golf is very demanding because of the time taken to play it: 4–8 hours for 18 or 36 holes, sometimes in temperatures at abnormal levels.

For your body to perform to a high level it is important to be reasonably fit as well as use the extra energy taken from food. This will help maintain an acceptable level of performance and keep you motivated.

Food gives the cells in the body essential energy. Nutrients found in food that provide the required energy are carbohydrates, protein, and fat. If the body is starved of these elements through long periods of exercise— such as 36 holes of golf—then the body will resort to eating its own fat and muscle in order for it to continuing functioning.

Carbohydrates

These should make up the majority of your daily energy intake and come in two forms:
● polysaccharides (starch)
● monosaccharides (glucose).

Starch plays a large role in exercise that takes a long period of time, such as a round of golf. Bread, potato, rice, and pasta will provide you with the starch you require. Your body will slowly break down this food into sugars which then enter the blood stream, allowing you to sustain exercise for longer periods of time. Glucose can be found naturally in honey, maple syrup, and fruits. It is also added to food such as candy, jams, and jelly. When these are digested, they are absorbed very quickly into the blood stream—unlike starches.

Protein

This is the smallest of the three nutrient sources in the way of daily energy intake, comprising only 10–15 percent of what you need. A lot of people see protein as a great way of developing muscles quicker and will eat more than the body actually requires. This can unbalance the body at the expense of displacing other nutritional needs, such as providing adequate levels of carbohydrates. Protein is often found in plants and animal products (meat, fish, eggs, and cheese). By having a healthy balance of protein you allow your body to grow, repair, and fight infections, and it is also able to carry oxygen to blood cells more effectively.

Fat

Unlike the other two nutrient sources, fat is harmful when you take too much on and it can cause long-term health problems such as heart disease, cancer, or even obesity. Fat should not make up any more than 25–30 percent of your daily energy intake. To reduce this percentage further from time to time is not a problem as long as you are eating a reasonable amount of carbohydrates when exercising. The body will always burn the carbohydrates first and will then, about 20 minutes into any exercise, start to use fat and fatty acids stored in the body which there is normally abundance of.

Diet for a golfer

It is always essential when playing golf for long periods of time to ensure your food comprises a good balance of protein with a higher carbohydrate intake and less fat than usual.

This will allow your body to use the carbohydrates correctly and will keep fat stores at a suitable level.

The healthiest way to absorb energy into your body is at meal times. If meals are consistent, they will provide your body with what it needs as and when it requires it.

You should always have some form of breakfast as this provides your body with the necessary energy levels to start the day, following the long period overnight when you haven't eaten. Breakfast is best eaten at least one hour before any form of exercise such as golf. During your breakfast and evening meal you should eat 50 percent of your daily energy intake.

Timing of food

When playing golf or doing some other form of exercise, your consumption should be little and often, thereby allowing your body to refuel and maintain its energy stores. Foods such as dried fruits cereal/energy bars or fruit cakes are perfect for maintaining this required energy during the day.

The body is most effective at refueling the muscles within the first two hours following exercise. With this in mind, a meal high in carbohydrate is optimal for the refueling process. Your breakfast and evening meal should be cooked and include hot drinks.

Tip

Mark a good golfing performance with a special meal. It need not necessarily be expensive or eaten at a restaurant, but it should enjoyable and healthy. Use food to help make the link between golf and pleasurable social events.

Training programs

Before you set your own training program for golf, you must understand how your body composition relates to your overall fitness level.

Body composition is the measured ratio of fat in relation to the body mass, and when this fat ratio is high you are considered overweight. This can be a cause of:

- heart disease
- diabetes
- back pain
- other health-related problems.

Therefore your weight may need to be reduced and monitored with regular physical exercise and good nutrition for a healthy body and a better game of golf.

Muscles needed in a golf swing

There are more than 20 muscles in use when creating a golf swing. They make up the lateral rotator movement of the hips, spine, shoulders, extensors of the forearms, and the wrist. A good understanding of the golf swing will allow you to feel the muscles being utilized. Therefore helping to develop each one so the muscle contracts quicker and thereby increases your ability to hit controlled powerful shots.

Before you physically enhance these muscle areas, you need to understand the following:

- specificity
- overload
- recovery
- adaptation
- reversibility.

Specificity

This is the ability to improve a range of movement within a particular area of the body. To gain full movement and the specific mobility requirements of the golf swing, you must test the range of movement to understand how it should be developed.

Overloading

An overloaded muscle will be strengthened only when it is forced to operate beyond its natural tolerance. The overload should be progressively increased to give a balanced, injury-free development. This increase is not always the need to run further or lift more weights. It can equate to running more often or increasing repetitions. As long as it is always gradual, training can be comfortable and progressive.

Recovery

Following a training session, your body needs rest to allow it to recover from the exertions.

Adaptation

After recovery, adaptations to the body are then allowed to take place, thereby increasing your muscle size and quality.

Reversibility

Whether you are just starting to train or have done so for a while, to stop exercising suddenly will have detrimental effects. Levels of aerobic endurance, muscular endurance, strength, and flexibility will reduce and body composition will increase. Reversibility is the reduction of certain exercise. You should therefore maintain all areas of personal development or else run the risk of undoing all the good that you have started.

Your program

The following are important considerations when building a training program to enhance your fitness for golf.

- Try to include three sessions a week dedicated to improving your fitness. Always ensure these sessions start with a cardio workout or are completely dedicated to a cardio workout.
- Try always to use free weights as this will give you more rounded core strength. Ensure these exercise work the whole body.
- Always include stretches in your exercise sessions, again concentrating on the full range of movement in all areas.
- When starting out on your exercise regime, schedule frequent short sessions with a light workload rather than occasional longer ones with a heavier workload. This will enable you to progress and improve at an appropriate pace. Do not try and do too much in a short space of time.
- Do not be afraid of getting out of breath. Allow this to happen as it is a sign of the lungs and heart working and should not be a concern if you have consulted a doctor or are comfortable with your own level of fitness.

Tip

Train with a partner. It is an established scientific principle that people performer better when in company. Pick someone who is just a little fitter than you to provide a challenge.

Golf exercises 1

This full range of rotational strength and core abdominal exercises for the whole body covers all areas needed to help with the golf swing movement.

When you decide to establish a program of exercise, always remember the following.

- warm up before exercise by very simple stretching
- quicken the heart rate by running on the spot
- starting gently with just a few repetitions; never overdo it
- do not set yourself impossible targets and if you miss sessions or fall behind your schedule, don't be too hard on yourself.

The ball used in many of the exercises is a standard medicine or stability ball. These come in different weights; choose one that is comfortable. Do not try to use one that is too heavy as you are exercising for strength and muscle toning—not to become a weightlifter.

Abdominal strengthening

To strengthen your abdominal muscles for golf, do this seated lateral twist exercise. Sit on the floor with your feet positioned slightly more than a shoulder's width apart. Grasp a stability ball to your chest with crossed hands. Then move it from one side to another by rotating your upper body but not your head.

The fact that you have to keep your head still in this exercise is also good preparation for the course.

Tip

Incorporate strength exercises into your daily life. Try holding muscles tighter for longer. Stand tall in queues, sit "strong" at your desk. Push carefully against resistance when you have the chance. Avoid slouching and unbalanced posture.

Ball swing

This is a standing exercise involving a smooth swinging action with a large ball. Stand with feet shoulder width apart with legs braced. The exercise should be completed slowly.

The starting position shown in image **A** requires you to move to position **B** and return to **A**. This should be repeated. Make sure you do the same for the other side, position **C** and **D**, and repeat in a flowing slow movement. Focus should be on achieving the maximum range available. This is an excellent activity for improving flexibility in the hips, back and shoulders.

A   B

C   D

These exercises use a smaller ball or weight. Try slow counting to make sure you complete the exercise rhythmically, not speeding up either the "backswing" or "follow through."

Back lift

The back lift allows for development of the muscles around in the lower spine. Care is required to avoid possible injury. It is recommended that this exercise is done after a thorough warm-up. You should begin slowly at first but the exercise can also be used to develop explosive power if required.

This is an exercise which will improve your all-important shoulder flexibility, so essential for effective golf. It also offers the opportunity to practice weight transference which is a key principle of producing accuracy with power in golf.

Choose a suitable ball for this exercise, only using the heavier one when you feel ready. Make sure the movement is smooth and continuous.

Golf exercises 2

Lateral passes

You need to maintain a fixed position to maximize the potential of this exercise. It is essential therefore, to produce an accurate pass. Face forwards to encourage a greater twisting movement of the hips. This also benefits your coordination and is an aid to concentration. Set targets for the numbers of successful catches to increase competitiveness.

Although golf is a "one-sided" sport your exercise regime should aim for all-round strength and flexibility. Do not favor one side so exercises such as the lateral pass should be done with equal repetitions on each side.

Tip

Incorporate flexibility into your daily life. Try reaching for things rather than going right up to them. See the difference when you come to do your exercises.

Swing resistance

Any exercise that allows you to develop the golf-specific movement is worthwhile but should not be too technical or a replacement of the actual swing. Swing fans and resistance bands are great tools for improving strength and flexibility.

The movement is the same as the golf swing from start to finish and should be repeated with the same number of repetitions on each side for complete body stability i.e. left and right handed swings.

Rotations

Rotations are excellent to help improve both shoulder and hip rotation, an area of flexibility having a direct impact on golfing success. Placement of your feet close together will increase the rotation potential and also test your balance. Keep your head high to ensure there is rotation around the spine only rather than forward bending.

Stand with your feet shoulder width apart, setting yourself up as you would with a golf shot. Your first movement should be to the top of your swing plane, returning past impact and continuing to the follow-through position. Start with a few slow swings until you're comfortable with increasing the speed, then repeat the movement several times.

This is an excellent warm-up exercise (shown here from different angles). Standing with feet apart feel the gentle stretching as you turn to each side.

Golf exercises 3

Functional Squat

Performing the functional squat effectively will improve overall body strength and stability (perfect for golf). To begin the squat you should stand in an upright position with your feet shoulder-width apart. Bend your hips then your knees, ensuring your knees stay behind your toes at all times. Hold your stomach muscles in tight during the movement and place your hands in front of you to offer stability. Concentration and controlled breathing are required throughout the movement. You may want to use the back of a chair to steady yourself the first time you try the functional squat. This exercise will offer a strong stable base for the golf swing.

This is one of the few exercises that doesn't reflect a natural part of your golf movement. However, it really will improve both flexibility and strength and aid the "walking tall" that you want to impose on your golf game.

Tip

Exercise of any kind is good for you and therefore good for your golf. Don't restrict yourself to a golf-specific regime. Remember to have golf goals in your mind when you are exercising—visualizing great shots, improved swing, better stamina etc. And finally, enjoy it. Always be grateful you can take exercise.

Lunge pass

With the lunge pass you are trying to develop flexibility around the pelvic area. The co-ordination of movement forward and the ball release will transfer to your swing and strike in golf. You can progress in this exercise through the depth of your lunge and the distance covered by the ball.

Start with the ball held simply in front before dipping and twisting to one side. Then, in one movement, swing back to release the ball, ideally throwing to a target or partner. The ball release must be from the crouched position as shown. Do equal reps for each side of course.

It is essential to keep the leading knee behind the toe when lunging forward to prevent injury. Exercise can be a solitary pursuit but using a partner not only provides the potential for more fun but is also likely to push you more than if exercising alone. Golfers often like both competition and an audience!

Equipment

If you *look* good on the golf course you will probably *feel* good too—and the importance of this perception is not to be underestimated. You will also want to own and use equipment in which you can develop trust. This will lead to confidence on the course and ultimately in the shots that need to be played.

Buying new clubs

There are probably two main questions to consider when thinking about new clubs. Is the technology going to change in the near future? Is my game going to change in the near future? Both answers may affect your decision.

Equipment upgrades

Technology moves the game on, but only by tiny increments, so be wary of jumping on the latest bandwagon. Whatever is the latest trend will almost certainly be yesterday's news a year or so later. There are numerous examples of top players going back to a favorite driver or putter in times of crisis, often with great success.

Also, note that the better the player, the less impact a technology change will make.

A professional could almost certainly play well with your clubs, no matter what they are. They might, however, play marginally better with their own, simply because they are completely confident and comfortable with them. The very latest driver would also work very well in a pro's hands, but for a crucial tournament winning drive they would probably want to have a tried and trusted club in their hands.

Finding the right clubs

Most golf stores offer a wide range of clubs and these will often be available to try. If you find a club that you like, buy it, even if it is the demo club. If you can't buy the demo make sure you try out a club which has been ordered for you before taking it away from the store as it could feel very different.

Don't get too hung up on terminology. Put what you feel is right in your bag. When you're facing a shot, choose the club that you feel can do the job. You can "drive" with any club off the tee and use your driver off the fairway. "Fairway"

woods can be invaluable out of light rough—and there's no problem in keeping a 7 or even 9 wood in your bag. The numerous hybrid clubs are exactly that—a "hybrid" of iron and wood.

Note their loft and shaft length (they may claim they are the equivalent of a particular iron or wood) and see how well and far they perform. Choose your woods or hybrids to suit you personally and then create a balanced bag for the course you are playing on the day.

There is so much on offer, and so much temptation, in golf equipment. How do you make a decision? Always test clubs out and always take advice from somebody you trust. You don't have to pay top dollar for perfectly good clubs and with the high turnover of styles there are often very good second-hand clubs and bags available.

Your changing needs

You can really only choose new clubs for that moment—to match how you are playing at the time of purchase. Therefore you need to think carefully about committing yourself before you have a round of lessons. Might your coach recommend a new swing, a different set-up? Although seemingly minor, this is an important point. You don't want to invest in a set of clubs that matched your old game and not your new.

Thinking about a fitting?

Rather than just buying off-the-shelf, having a fitting will certainly make you more comfortable and confident with your clubs. You will know that the clubs you hold are the right flex, height, grip, weight etc. for your game. This is not to say you can't play perfectly well with other clubs—but you just may not be so confident. The better the fitting the quicker the personal development will be.

Asking the right questions

Before doing anything, and especially before spending any money, do ask yourself these questions.

- Do I need a full set of clubs immediately or could I just find one fitted golf club to practise with first?
- Am I ready for a new set of golf clubs or am I making any big change to my swing in the near future?
- Do I need a fitting? Am I swinging well but getting lots of different ball flight results that I can't explain?

Bags and trolleys

Just as with new club selection there are fundamental questions to ask—and answer—before buying a new bag or trolley. The most important of these, and a question that many golfers ignore, is exactly what should go in your bag.

A common sight, and a distraction for both players and partners, is a golfer laboring under an enormous golf bag, bursting with extras that are often impossible to find. It is even worse when you are carrying the bag and you should have it on a trolley.

Sort out what you need to take on the course and then select your bag and/or trolley to match. Don't choose your bag and then see what you can fit in it.

Bag contents

Settle on what you really need to take out with you; the decision about the bag and trolley will follow-on naturally:

- clubs—to suit the course and your game
- balls—type, how many?
- gloves—type, how many?
- tees, markers
- refreshments—liquids, foods (is there water on the course?)
- clothing—cold/wet weather kit, overtrousers, studs
- umbrella, bag cover
- extras—suntan lotion or lip creams, sunglasses, towel, etc.

A professional's bag is geared to make the playing of the game as easy as possible; make yours the same.

Carrying a bag

Should you decide that you can manage all your equipment in a bag, you should also think about the following:

- use as lightweight a bag as you can
- use a cross-over strap that evens up the weight of the bag
- ensure that the straps are evenly adjusted laterally
- hold the bag high up the back and quite tightly; it must not be low or loose around the lower back
- put your extra weight (balls etc.) as near the bottom of the bag as possible to balance them with your club heads
- make sure your bag does not have any pockets, clips, or straps that will rub your back
- on a padded bag make sure the straps are tight enough to position the padding in line with your back.

With a carry bag you can walk directly to the ball and do not have to take detours around greens and other parts of the course where trolleys are banned. Carrying fewer than 14 clubs in practice rounds will also make you focus on aspects of shot-making much more carefully.

Bigger bags and trolleys

If you opt for a large bag, do try to have as many pockets as you can. These can each take separate items—balls, gloves, water etc.—which makes life much easier when out on the course.

Then you have to decide on the types of trolley: push, pull, or powered. Dragging a heavy trolley and bag, from one side or the other, especially over a long round, can seriously affect your spine, so it is generally best to push your trolley, even if it is a pull design. Using a powered trolley means that

you can arrive at the ball fresh for your next shot. If you intend to play 36 holes in one day, or are playing several days in a row, then a powered trolley is probably ideal.

If you play your golf from a buggy or electric cart then the problem of fatigue is even less. The only drawback with electric carts can be that you may have to leave them some way from your ball. If this is the case, take plenty of clubs with you to the ball. If you stand over the ball and think you don't have the correct club do not compromise. Go back and get the right club from you bag.

Woods selection

It is important to understand why you need certain clubs.
The driver has one main purpose—to gain as much distance as
possible with control and accuracy. If this can be achieved then you
can feel confident about trying to hit the safe area in the fairway. It
is much the same with the fairway woods, but here distance control
as well as accuracy are more important.

The driver

There are so many new developments that it is
hard to keep pace with what is best. When
choosing a new driver, perhaps the ideal policy
is to understand what each driver offers but
select the one with which you feel most
confident, as no two clubs are the same when
taken off the shelf.

Driver head

There are certain factors to consider about a
driver head.

- Research what head makes you feel
  comfortable to look down at and to align to
  your selected target.
- Find a head shape and size that are pleasing
  to the eye. Different shaped heads may
  allow you to change your ball flight. Do not
  be drawn into the modern gimmicks without
  trying them first.
- Check out the driver's loft. Too many golfers
  play with too little loft, which often will cost
  them a loss of distance and accuracy. More
  loft equals more control of your ball flight.
- Consider the material of any wood as this
  has evolved quickly in the past 15 years.
  Manufacturers have developed light bigger
  heads that offer greater playability than the
  traditional wooden heads.

Shaft flex

This allows the player to find their optimum
ball flight and power without compromising
accuracy. Shafts are available in a range of
materials and flexes to accommodate these
requirements for all levels of ability.

*Test it out, make a decision and be happy with
the decision. And always take time with a new
driver; it's unlikely you will hit your best ever
shots immediately after a purchase.*

The kick point is where the shaft flexes, and it will vary between high, mid, and low. Shafts that are designed for a lower ball flight will tend to have higher kick point, while those designed for a higher ball flight will have a lower kick point.

Height and flex

It's more important to get the lie angle correct than that tall players should have longer shafts. Often the change in length of shaft will effect performance: the longer the shaft, the more flex is added. You can choose a shorter shaft which might offer you more control over the club. What is fundamental when considering any club is that you find the right club that gives you the best posture set-up and the potential to develop your swing further.

Driver grip

And don't forget the grip, whether cord, rubberized, fat, or thin… there are no rules. Just choose what you feel comfortable with. But do remember to maintain the grip as carefully as the rest of the club. Clean, or

eventually replace the grip, when necessary. Never ask for thick grips; instead always request more tape to be put onto the shaft before covering with the grip. This will keep the club light and so retain its feel and performance. It is worthwhile lightly rubbing corded grips with an abrasive paper from time to time as this removes the rubber, allowing the cord to come back to the surface.

Fairway woods

These woods are not just for fairway shots; they can also be used off the tee and out of the rough. There is no magic formula for choosing your club or clubs but you might want to:

- think about the overall balance of your bag
- match the materials, weight, and style of your driver
- ensure you are not duplicating distance and usefulness with an iron or hybrid.

Most of all, use clubs that give you confidence. Look forward to employing the best tools for the job.

The hybrid

Hybrids (sometimes called utility clubs or transition irons) were originally so-called because they contained two materials in the head. Today the name implies an iron-style club face with a wood-style bulb behind. Most manufacturers claim hybrids are easier to hit as they have shorter shafts than their iron equivalents, and so they promote them to replace the longer irons (about 5 iron upwards). Most professionals will have a hybrid in their bag.

You need to try them out, decide where they work for you, and put them in your bag as required. They are not a magic solution but neither are they simply a gimmick.

Sometimes you may hear the term "rescue club." These are hybrids with more weight built into the sole of the club to give greater distance.

Irons

With your irons you are trying to provide complete cover of distance from, say, 100 to 200 yards. Shorter than this and you might be looking at wedges, longer and you might start thinking about hybrids or woods. The pitching wedge, 9, 8, 7, 6, 5, and 4 iron are the main core of an iron "set." The 1, 2, and 3 iron are all usable, but are now mostly replaced by hybrids or woods. Many manufacturers don't actually make these long irons as standard any more.

Comfort is the key

As with woods, it is important you choose the irons you feel comfortable with. If you can hit a set of irons consistently your confidence will soar and both your shot making and course management will improve enormously.

When trying out new clubs on the range, always hit naturally with a full swing. This is what you will be aiming for on the course. Also note the distances of each iron.

Whether you choose your pitching wedge to match your irons is up to you. Some golfers match their pitching wedge with the rest of their wedges. Do try out high irons (if you can get them) but remember the hybrid or wood alternatives.

Club fitters and golf companies will try to balance the loft of all the clubs so that you are not presented with any gaps in your distance. This should provide a club for every situation and an even set of distances between one club and the next. What this does not take into account is your short game. It will be up to you to alter your shot, or choose from your wedges, to play, for example, a bump and run, a chip, pitch, or lob shot.

Don't expect miracles the first time you use your new irons. There is a tendency to try too hard. Swing slowly, watch the ball, and be confident that you will get there.

The most important factor when searching for the right irons and wedges is finding the correct lie angle—getting this wrong can have a serious affect on your ability to hit the ball correctly. The correct lie angle means the sole of the club head sits flat on the ground when static and, ideally, when dynamic at impact. If the club head is too upright you will produce a pull or hook because the club will close at impact with the ground. If the club head is too flat then expect the face to open and a push or slice of the ball to occur. Both factors will make an uneven divot mark which is normally a good indicator for you to have your clubs' lie angles checked.

Most golfers have the wrong lie angles on their clubs and would just gain from having these checked much more than any other areas of custom fitting.

Knowing the jargon

When you listen to the salesman or read the literature you may be faced with a wealth of information. You don't need to know everything but you can be prepared. All of these words apply to irons and many of them relate to other clubs as well.

- **Bounce** allows the club to make minimal impact with the ground, preventing the club head from digging into the ground. This becomes a more important feature on wedges as these are often the clubs that require the most precision when playing a shot. Bounce angle needs can be very different when playing a links course as opposed to a parkland.

- **Cavity back** is a scooped-out back which moves the weight around the perimeter of the club head. This makes the club more forgiving with off-centre hits.

- **Club head** speed varies from one club to the next, so it will play an important part when you are being fitted with your clubs. It could determine the type of shaft you need to find distance and control.

- **Launch angle** is often confused with the club head angle. It actually refers to the angle at which the ball leaves the club head. If it is too high or too low the ball could lose distance.

- **Lie angle** plays an important part in allowing the clubs to be custom fitted to the individual. The lie angle must suit your swing; if not, you may lose distance or cause the ball to go in the wrong direction.

- **Loft** varies between clubs and causes the ball on each club to fly a different trajectory and distance.

- **Offset** should assist you in squaring the club head up at impact. With the head set back from the shaft there is more time for the head to get into the correct position. This feature will suit those who generally hit a cut. The launch angle will reduce because the shaft is positioned in front of the head.

- **Pure-ing** has become very popular with the modern Tour player as they search for perfection in their bag. Shaft pure-ing is a technique used to determine the correct shaft alignment in relation to the head. This process allows for optimum performance from the individual shaft.

- **Shaft** changes will allow you to find the optimum ball flight and power without compromising accuracy. Shafts are available in a range of materials and flexes to accommodate these requirements for all ages and abilities. At impact, a correctly fitted shaft will increase your chance of maximum energy transfer into the ball.

- **Ball spin** allows the ball to hook, fade, slice, or draw, which might help you play the course more efficiently. Spin is created by the club face being open or closed to the swing path at impact. By shaping a shot, the ball will increase or decrease in distance, and so this factor will have to be taken into account when selecting your club.

Wedges

By the time you choose your wedges you should have a good idea of what you are hoping to achieve with them. Having settled on the purpose of the clubs, the selection process should be relatively straightforward. Even though there are names for the various wedges—pitching, sand, gap, lob etc.—it's probably best to think in terms of degrees of elevation.

Sets of wedges

Club fitters are likely to promote an equal divide between one loft of a club to the next and this will be done with a three- or a four-wedge combination. There is always pressure to sell bundles of clubs rather than just one at a time:

- Typical **four-wedge combination**
  46, 50, 54, 58 degrees
  48, 52, 56, 60 degrees
- Typical **three-wedge combination**
  46, 52, 58 degrees
  48, 54, 60 degrees

The angle is relative to vertical, not to the ground. A high-lofted club, such as a sand wedge, will be at the high end of the elevation scale, somewhere around 55 degrees. So-called lob wedges can go as high as you choose (there's no limit within the rules of golf) but generally about a 60-degree loft is needed for a perfect flop shot.

You can choose a "set" from one manufacturer or put together your own combination. Choose wedges for the courses you are playing on.

Choosing whether you go for a higher or lower degree set depends on your game and the courses you most frequently play. To be able to focus more on the lower shots into the green you should consider a four-wedge combination of 46, 50, 54, and 58 degrees. For high softer shots into the green, select

wedges with elevations of, for example, 48, 55, 57, and 60 degrees.

Both set-ups still offer the ability to hit full shots and you still need to know what wedge offers what distance. But choosing higher or lower angles fine-tunes your game to your requirements.

Bounce

Professional or complete beginner, all golfers should consider playing with bladed wedges. It is easy to be drawn into buying a set of irons complete with the wedges, all with cavity backs. Trying to play light touch shots around the green with control is very difficult when you have an oversized wedge in your hand.

Some manufacturers are putting increased bounce on their wedges but too much bounce can raise the club leading edge off the ground and possibly cause a thin. If you open the club head more to the target to increase the loft of the club, the separation of that leading edge will increase further from the ground reducing your ability to play creative shots. Your aim: try to play with minimal bounce and see how easy it is to get the club head under the ball; this will increase your ability and control of the shot.

The bounce angle on a sand wedge again does not need to be too high. A wider sole is what you need when opening the face of the club in a bunker. Also consider other high lofted clubs to assist with the great escape from that unwanted trap.

The use of wedges depends on a range of factors including not only the target and distance but also the ground conditions. Padraig Harrington chips onto a green from fairly hard, unforgiving ground—also taking into account the slight slope.

Modern clubs tend to have rounded, not flat, soles. This lessens the amount of contact of the club with the ground.

It's all relative

Discover your natural style of game around the green and then choose your wedges around that style. There is very little point finding what wedges go what distance when you can never really know what your approach shots are going to be. There is more of a need for the little touch shots around the green than there is for the full shot.

Putters

Is the putter the most important club that can be found in the bag? It's certainly the one that will be used more than any other, perhaps as much as 45 percent of your shots. With the possible exception of the driver, it is probably the one club that needs to be used with total confidence. Once you start blaming your putter you're in trouble.

Putters built around you

Loft—This is the angle needed on the putter face to get the ball up and rolling across the surface of the putting green; the slower the green the more loft that is required and on a faster green less loft is needed. On most putters the loft is 2–4 degrees. At impact the dynamic loft of the putter is the most important thing to consider over and above the static loft, this is the true loft of the putter.

Lie angle—This is how upright or flat a putter is when the club is sitting parallel on the putting surface. The standard lie angle of 19 degrees is far too upright for most players, and a lie angle of 21 degrees will allow your arms to work more naturally under your shoulders.

Toe hang—The putter has the heaviest part of its mass positioned in the toe, which allows it to hang down. This promotes better rotation just after impact as the heavy toe wants to keep moving as the putter slows down. This often suits a better player with a smooth stroke.

Putter head face inserts—These create a totally different reaction to the ball off the putter face. A balata-type insert gives a softer slower release of the ball off the face, while a harder face such as stainless steel provides a faster release of the ball. The addition of various designs of face grooves can reduce skid and improve the roll of the ball.

Putter head—This is one of the most important components of a putter. Putter heads are available in many blade designs—centre-shafted, mallets, small, large, light, heavy, with inserts and without—and many different materials.

Different heads and inserts.

Grip size—For personal comfort it is important that the putter grip should fit your particular hand and finger size or grip technique. Ladies and juniors usually require a smaller grip size than a fully mature man.

Grips vary in both shape and thickness.

Grip shape—This very individual aspect of a putter is determined purely on feel. Some people prefer a grip with soft rounded lines, while others are happier with much harsher sharper features.

Toe and heel weighting—The weight is concentrated at both ends of the putter head. This is part of all good putter design as it allows the sweet spot of your putter to be as forgiving as possible on off-centre hits of the golf ball.

Hosel offset—The putter has an angled, S-shaped neck called a hosel between the shaft and the head, so the shaft can be set anywhere from level with the putter face to up to 12mm (approx 0.5ins) forward of the putter face. An offset toe-and-heel putter can make a significant difference to your ability to aim the putter face to the target correctly. To determine whether you need a putter with offset, ask a pro to measure the amount of added loft or deloft at impact.

Centre shafted—This putter normally has a balanced face and its shaft is mounted directly in the centre of the putter head. Alternatively the hosel is set to allow the putter shaft to run

through the centre line of the putter face, both maintaining an equal balance between the toe and heel. On some putters that have weighting systems this can be changed by adding heavier or lighter weights to make the toe come up or down, to suit your stroke mechanics.

Length—The shaft length should suit your personal profile, enabling you to stand in correct relationship to the ball time after time. Shaft length is determined not only by your height but also, often more, by the lengths of your arms and legs. Therefore you can often find a tall player will require just as short a putter as a person that is nowhere near as tall.

Shaft and butt weighting—The overall dead weight of your putter as well as its swing weight can be adjusted, even though the swing weight of a putter is nothing like as important as that of the rest of the clubs in the bag. By adding butt weighting you are counter-balancing the putter and decreasing the swing weight; you are also moving the centre of gravity, i.e. the balance point. By adding a heavier shaft you will increase your putter's overall weight and create a stiffer feel, with less flex in the shaft.

The angle of shaft and head can also be built around you.

Putters... and balls

Although club choice is a question of confidence, it's advisable to use a standard putter if you can. Other types are of minority interest.

More about putters

Players that use non-standard putters are often experimenting with ways of keeping the club as still as possible by anchoring the shaft to the body.

Standard putter

This allows you to lean over the ball when putting. The standard putter is available in a range of shaft lengths and lie angles, to suit you personally. Both feature changes should enable you to drop your hands, palm to palm, around the putter's grip.

The broom-handle putter

This long-handled putter enables you to take hand movement largely out of the equation when striking the ball. You will create a complete pendulum in an upright stance. The broom handle does mean considerable loss of feel on the shot. A putt becomes totally mechanical and takes a lot of getting used to.

The belly putter

The belly putter encourages a more natural putting stroke and gives you a stabilizing factor for your putt, namely the abdomen. If you have ever suffered from the "yips," or even just slightly shaky hands, the belly putter may work for you. The putter is anchored against the body, and wrist action is easier to control. The disadvantages might be lack of touch and, possibly, lack of speed control.

You can play up to 45 per cent of your shots with a putter so spend a proportionate amount of time choosing the style that suits you. Here Ian Woosnam putts for birdie, using his broom-handle putter, on the first hole during the third round of the 2008 US Senior Open Championship.

Choosing your golf ball

The golf ball is the centre of the game, the single most important bit of equipment one needs on the golf course. Today there are four types of ball, ranging from one-piece to four piece.

The one-piece is normally sold at the lower end of the market or found on golf ranges. The two- and three-piece (together with the most recent four-piece) are so called depending upon the number of layers. In general the greater the number of layers, the softer the ball feels. Assuming you have an average swing speed, a two-piece ball should be the ideal choice, but don't be put off thinking that three-piece balls are not for you.

There is a temptation to think that the harder balls, giving more distance off the tee, are better for higher handicap golfers. Remember however, that in a typical round you may play 14 drives but numerous chips and putts. Certainly to play any

ball that has three or more layers in its make up will require you to control the ball spin better and increase compression at impact but it may be worth sacrificing 14 times 10 yards for that much greater feel around the greens.

Of course, play with different balls to find what suits your swing speed and game. Within a wide range of manufacturers' balls, despite their claims, you will probably not notice enormous differences in actual performance, although you will notice the different feel of club on ball. With many new drivers you will also notice a different sound!

Ultimately choose a type of ball that you play well with and stick with it for a while. When your game is having a down turn think about changing.

It won't be the ball's fault but it might make you feel better and help regain that all-important confidence.

When taking out your practice bag try to use the same type of ball you use on the course particularly when honing your short game.

Other equipment

It's tempting to neglect the value of some of the other items in your bag. However, golf is a game of small margins, and you really need every advantage you can find. If the correct tee or use of a towel gives you a shot here and there it's worth taking the trouble over their selection and inclusion.

Tees are used for raising the ball off the ground to allow the club head to swing through the ball with no resistance. This is the key. Find the right length tee for the shot, ensuring that it does not sit in the ground too far. A useful tip is to find a soft part of the teeing area—don't anchor the tee in so hard it will never move.

A **towel** is important just to keep club grips dry and balls and blades clean. Don't forget to keep it relatively clean. You might like to store an additional towel inside your umbrella, so, when it is raining, you know that at least this towel is kept dry.

A small **club head cleaner** will enable you to clean club faces and keep groves free from dirt. Keep one in your pocket and get into the routine of using it regularly.

Using a combined **scorecard and yardage book holder** will mean that the card and yardage book is more accessible when walking round the course. It will also keep them dry.

Although you think you know the rules, there are often occasions when you wish you had a **rule book** to refer to. Situations arise and you need to be certain. If you have the answer to hand then you can put the situation behind you and concentrate on the next shot.

Experiment with different tees until you find the one that gives you most confidence but don't forget you'll need your ball at different heights for different shots.

You can often see professionals or their caddies cleaning clubs after every shot, especially as the players often take a divot with each stroke. Don't allow your clubs to become encrusted with mud and dirt. Taking care of your clubs by cleaning them regularly is essential.

Finding your yardage

Any item that can be used for counting or calculating distance is always good to have. These may include a clicker, toggles, a range finder, or a sophisticated GPS (Global Positioning System).

The low-tech **clickers** (which count paces) is helpful if used with care.

A **range finder** calculates the distance you have left to your given target. Note that these will vary in accuracy.

Accurate—if calibrated to the course correctly—and easy to use, this navigation system certainly gives you every chance of making an informed club selection. Many clubs have them built into buggies, and hand-held varieties are also available. Three points, however: Make sure you know where the GPS is measuring (to the middle or front of the green); remember to note where the flag is; and check out whether you can use it in any competition in which you are playing.

Many professionals use a rangefinder in their practice rounds. Here Morgan Pressel checks her yardage for her second shot using a rangefinder at the 6th hole during the pro-am preview for the 2008, Kraft Nabisco Championship.

What to wear

Golf has always had a flamboyant image with players
marching around the countryside in their plus fours and long socks.
This originated from the need to be dressed appropriately for all
weathers and terrain. Today "golf fashion" is at its height with
elaborate (and often expensive) clothing available from most golf
clubs, golf stores and the Internet. The advice, however, remains
unchanged. Think "playing comfort, weather protection and course
etiquette," in that order.

Gloves

Remember the reason for a glove, to provide a
better grip especially when sweating or when
your club is wet. When choosing, always go
for a relatively tight glove. You don't have to
wear just one glove; you can wear a pair of
gloves if this feels comfortable. Comfort and
confidence are key. Leather gloves are
hardwearing. Those that claim to be "all-
weather" are more water resistant and warm
but they are only thin gloves; they can't work
miracles.

In wet weather carry spare gloves—in cold
weather wear over-mittens between shots.
Cold hands can mar your ability to make a
good shot.

Shoes

Comfort is crucial but so is grip. There should
be no thoughts in your mind about slipping as
you prepare to drive. You need a solid anchor.
So sturdy uppers and good spikes or cleats are
important. Many clubs will specify soft spikes
or cleats to be worn so these might be a better
purchase if you can't afford two pairs of
shoes—although you can change cleats to suit
the surface and the weather.

Clothing

You know what you like but think comfort and
confidence. Looking good will probably make
you feel good. In practical terms you might
prefer the short sleeved tops for freedom of
movement. It's worth spending money on
getting good, breathable, waterproofs. And
waterproof trousers, rather than waterproof
over trousers, are a good idea. They are
warm, smart, keep you dry and you don't
have to keep pulling them on and off in
changeable weather.

When purchasing water and windproofs
remember they should:
- be wind proof
- keep water out
- keep heat in
- allow vapour to escape.

You can probably get away with your legs
getting cold or wet but it's your body core that
you must protect. The less you look after this
the more body heat and energy you are likely
to use which generally leads to a reduction in
performance. Be aware that a waterproof will
always be windproof the opposite is not
always true.

Layers

If it is to be a particularly cold day have it in your mind to wear several layers of clothes. This will offer you the option of increasing layers as and when you need them. During a round you may find air temperature changes as well as your body temperature. You can't swing freely and well if you are cold.

In cold or wet weather the availability of layers of clothes provides flexibility, but also a heavier bag. In bad weather it's probably best to turn to a powered trolley.

Caps hats and visors

How can such small items save you shots? Remember shaded eyes can be an important factor when looking to see where your ball is going to land. More importantly a head covering allows you to retain up to 35% of your body heat. On this subject, sunglasses may also be a good investment but don't wear them for the first time in an important match. Get used to them first—see how much light they stop.

Finally, don't forget good sun block. Spending four hours or so exposed to the elements can have adverse effects on your skin, both short and long term.

Practice

We practice so that we can improve. Practice should always have a purpose, which will provide the goal. With goals you can measure your achievement. And it can also be fun!

Mental drill

As you know, golf is a game played by the body and the
mind. There are numerous ways to practice the former—but it's not
so easy to *practice* the latter. In trying to train the brain you need to
trick it so it believes it really is involved in a real match, on the
course. In this way you can practice establishing the right mental
pitch for that next big match.

Playing the course on the range

This exercise is about the visualizing what
needs to be done on the course. If you allow
yourself to be submerged into this exercise
you will feel as if you're on the course,
calculating your every move.

Simply start by imagining you are
standing on the tee of the 1st hole. Calculate
where your attack point or reactive target
(see page 164) should be and then play the
shot as if you were on the course. You will
know how well you have played the ball and
you should know what the lie of the land will
do to your ball; work out how the ball will
react to the shot you have just hit and figure
where the ball may have landed if that same
shot was played on the actual course. Once
you have done this simply play your next shot
from where you have estimated your landing
would be. Then take the appropriate club and
play this second shot.

There is no need to putt with this exercise
but do count your shots; add on two putts
for every hole unless you feel you have
knocked it very close. Repeat this for all 18
holes and log your score every time you finish
a hole. This exercise gives real focus to your
practice and encourages you to think about

every shot. Importantly too it stops you
rushing into your next shot on the tee as you
will have to change clubs each time.

Tip
Take your time over every shot and don't give up
if you score badly on a couple of holes.

*It's easy to hit a lot of wasted balls on the range. Think
about every shot. Make them all count. Playing the
course on the range is a great drill before a round of
golf, to get you truly focused on the game at hand.*

Play line

This drill is to help you learn to turn on, as well as turn off, on the course. The "play line" in question is an imaginary point of no return. You actually use this drill with every shot you play when on the course… but you may not use it well.

The play line can be called the commitment line—once crossed there is no return. If you imagine a line between you and the ball then, once the line has been crossed, you must move that ball on. What you need to do before you cross the line is plan *where* you want to move the ball to and *how* you will get it there.

Once you have made a firm decision and are committed to that in your head you are ready to cross the play line. Once the line has been crossed, the only thing you should have in your head is the target that you are aiming for. You will be free of technical information, "what ifs," doubts. You can focus on the target and let everything else be natural and instinctive.

Even in a social game try to make the most of the opportunity to play golf. Crossing the play line is a personal drill which can be used to focus your attention without your partner or opponent's knowledge. Used throughout the game, this drill can help maintain concentration.

Such a drill, used in friendly games as well as matches, will sharpen up your course management as well as providing practice in focus and concentration. Importantly it will help you turn on and off. You cannot concentrate totally over a three- to four-hour round. Having lines to cross, times to sharpen up your concentration, and times to take it easy will help balance your round.

Practice point

As it is hard to concentrate totally for an 18-hole round of golf, you need to be able to relax, and concentrate, at the appropriate times. Make practice the same. Talk to your coach, stand down, relax… and then go into your own zone of concentration. Emulate, as far as possible, the match scenario.

Tip

If using this technique in a social round don't tell your partners; just try to ignore the distractions.

Putting

Putting can be the most nerve-wracking part of the game— perhaps with the exception of the 1st tee shot watched by lots of other people! An important key in practising putting is to emulate, as far as possible, the real match situation. Although this is not entirely possible there is no substitute for introducing an element of competition into your practice. If you can work with another player, good, but sometimes it's important to spend time alone, focusing on one aspect of your putting.

Pull back

Mark a line to the hole six tees set three feet apart. This will give you an 18-foot line. With this drill you are required to play three balls from three foot location and try to hole all three balls (remember to focus on a real or imaginary tee that you can see pressed into the back of the hole).

This drill prevents you from hitting from the same spot excessively. It's good to have "new" putts each time. If you use a technique such as aligning your ball markings or plumb lining in a match continue to do the same in practice.

If you can hole two or more putts, then you can move to the next station which will take you to six feet. If, however, you do not achieve two putts or more then you need to continue to putt from that same station until you can move back. If this happens at a more distant tee, move forward taking three feet off your distance until you are putting consistently well from there. Then move back to the next three-foot station. You should keep doing this until you reach eighteen feet which will bring the game to an end. If you tell yourself you can't finish until you've completed the drill then you have introduced your own degree of competition.

This game will teach you to control your distance, developing feel for the putt.

Remember to focus on the back of the hole for every shot as this will allow your instinct to take over.

Tip

It is good to add variety to this drill. Try working on uphill and downhill lies, and across the slope.

Practice point

Whenever practising putting it is useful to mark the back of a hole with a tee (make sure not to damage the hole). This will keep your focus on this as your target. It should encourage positive putting.

On the practice green there is often plenty going on, so try to stay focused and not be distracted by how well your opponents are putting! Also you ought to try to check whether the practice green is the same pace as the actual greens.

Indirect putting

This drill allows you to work on both long and short putts. The idea with your first ball is to miss the hole to the side by between two feet and four feet. If you need to, use a tee peg to mark the four foot boundary.

The first shot should see you about two feet away from the hole but no more than four feet. Your first shot is all about pace; you will not have lined up for the hole. This leads onto your second shot, holing out.

With this shot align yourself and make the putt count. This will test your nerve on the shorter putts and will also give you a realistic chance of working on your alignment. This is a good drill to play against another player, perhaps over nine holes. You lose a point if your second putt does not go in the hole.

You get one point for the hole if you achieve the sequence of putts (up to the distance and then in the hole). You lose a point if your first putt is either too close or too far away.

Tip

Set a target (say nine holes) and stick with it; there is less focus with an open-ended game. With all practice stay with targets and aim to achieve set goals.

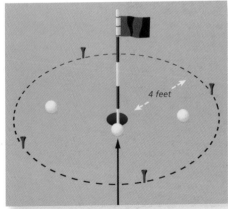

Indirect putting—the only time in golf where you are not trying to sink the first putt!

The short game

Putting practice is easy to organize, and drives and long iron shots can readily be played from the range. It is the short game that is hardest to practice—yet it is probably the area in which you need most work. Professionals work endlessly on the short game as the number of times they get "up and down" from just off the green proves. Take time to work on *your* short game; you will be rewarded.

Tunnel

This is a game that needs you to set-up on the short games area using either sticks or golf clubs. Lay the clubs/sticks about two feet apart, running parallel to each other and funeling toward the hole.

Depending upon the type of shot (pitch, chip, or bump and run shots probably) you are playing you will soon recognize the length required. Make sure at least one pair of sticks or clubs are close to the ideal landing spot. Feel free to set the clubs up to accommodate breaks in the green as this will improve your understanding of line and pace.

Play your shots toward the hole, fine-tuning the target as you observe how the ball rolls. You can create a scoring system if you wish to compete with yourself and others.

Tip

Note the relative difference in targets between the different types of shot; this will help in shot selection, especially when you have a tricky pin position.

lofted shots

chip and run shots

Place the clubs close to where you intend to pitch the ball, closer to the pin for lofted shots, further away for chip and run. Challenge yourself—reducing the space between the clubs will test your accuracy.

Par 18

This ideally should be played on a short game area that offers plenty of surrounding space. Set up a total of nine locations outside the green for you to play your shot from. Once you have this in place then you are ready to start.

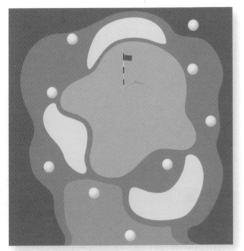

There is a temptation to spot the ball in games like this. Don't be tempted; play it as it lies.

Using one ball start from your first location and hit the ball as close to the hole as you can, then try to make the putt. If you get the ball up and down, then this will count as a par. If you have three shots or more then this will count as one or two to over par. Keep a matchplay-style score. Your aim is to go round all the locations in 18 shots or fewer. If you can achieve close to this, be more creative with your nine locations, perhaps moving them further away from the green or behind obstacles. The better you get the further out you go.

Tip

Try just one club and one type of shot (pitch, chip etc.) in one practice session. Play until you feel confident before changing to another.

Don't ignore distance when working on the range. Use the markers provided to judge your shots' range as well as accuracy.

Practice point

Playing the game is good practice, no matter what type of "match" you are involved in. If your nephew asks you to take him to the range or your partner wants to go on a local par-3 course—use the time constructively. You will have the chance to practice a variety of shots, very frequently short-game shots, that you may need in more serious situations later. Don't just throw opportunities away—and make sure you beat your family members!

The swing

The range is the best place to practise the swing. The danger of the range is that a bucket of balls can be fired off very quickly with little or no thought... sometimes even compounding errors in your game. Always take care to set-up properly, checking grip, stance, and alignment on every shot. Also look carefully at the tee mats and targets to ensure that they are aligned. If not, set yourself up accordingly.

Ball shaping

Ball shaping as a skill is a difficult thing to master but you need to feel and understand the difference between what it takes to hit a straight shot as opposed to a draw or fade. In this drill you start with a 9 or 8 iron, first hitting a straight shot then a draw followed by a fade. This will give you a total of three balls per club.

Then move onto the next club in your bag. You can do this 8–9 times with a total of 8–9 clubs, irons, woods, and hybrids included, giving you a total of 24–27 balls to play. Score yourself a point for every shot you pull off. Just make sure you know what shot you intend to hit; do not make this choice after you have played the shot—be fair to yourself. Give this exercise your time and patience and watch how easy it is to master and replicate these shots over time.

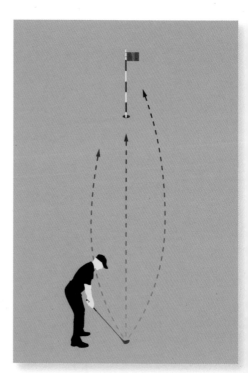

Ball shaping is well worth practising—it is not rocket science. Apart from set-up and execution you are trying to feel what it takes to produce a draw or fade.

Tip
Always start this exercise with a short iron and work up, not the other way round.

Avenue

This is a simple exercise that will keep you focused when playing shots on the range, practising and monitoring both direction and club distance. Simply start with a sand wedge and work through the bag until you get to the driver. The idea of this exercise is to hit each ball inside an "avenue," two lines that run adjacent to each other down the range with a reasonable distance between them. This avenue can change in size, generally getting smaller the better you get at it. Perhaps start with a 15-yard target.

There are 48–52 points to be gained, a single point for every shot that lands in the avenue; if the ball misses left or right you cannot count this as a point scored. Hit four balls with each club starting with the sand wedge as this will develop confidence. Do this with 12 or 13 clubs, which will give you the total of 48–52 shots.

Do not just use this exercise to record your points every time; also look at where you are missing and count how many times you miss right or left. This will help fault-find errors in your swing. Also make a mental check of your distances as this will allow you to adjust to the seasonal changes that affect the ball. If you need to create an avenue, ask if you can move the flags, or use some flour and pour this down the range. It is worth having a real, rather than imagined, target if at all possible.

To increase the value of your practice time keep records of your efforts so you can monitor areas of need and improvement.

Tip

Remember to check the type of range ball you are using when measuring distance. Some may be softer than the ball you normally use and may not carry as far.

Practice point

Go to the range for your practice as a separate process from warming up. In your warm-up you are looking to get your body working physically, play a wide variety of shots, and prepare mentally. This is different from practice. In practice sessions you should have different goals and specific targets.

On the course

It would be hard to spend too much time on the range and practice green—there is always something to work on—but remember also how important it is to practise on the course. There is no substitute for having real trees, bunkers, and terrain in your eye line. The two drills here are both based on nine holes, intended for when you are on your own. However you can build practice into every non-competition round, trying out different shots and pushing your safety limits to see what might be possible in the future.

Par 27

This is a game that will offer a greater understanding of how to attack the greens on the course. This game is best played over nine golf holes and should be quicker than the traditional nine holes played. The game is simple: just choose a distance between 70 and 180 yards (unless there is a short par-3) and play the course from that distance on all nine holes.

You can add in an element of course management too. For example, play from 110 yards away and choose the best location to come in from, as this will allow you to understand how to set your attack points (see page 166).

Once you have chosen your location, play the hole

out and record your score; this will keep you focused and also allow you to see parts of your course you may never have played shots from before.

If you can do this exercise with a range of distances and record your scores, then this will build up a clear picture of holes you are weak on or distances you need to work on.

Keep the distance the same for each hole, only change this when you play on a different day. This will give you a chance to play the same approach distance nine times, giving you an understanding of how clubs work for different holes and how they will react on different greens.

Tip

Don't play this game defensively. Attack every flag—and remember to hole out everything.

Plus-one

This is another game played over nine golf holes and is particularly useful for your short game. The plan is to hit the green in one extra shot. Thus, if you are on a par-4 you're allowed to hit three shots before you put the ball on the green. Try to get the ball as close to the green as you can before taking that extra shot, then focus on that short game, try to get the ball as close to the flag as you can.

If you one putt the ball on a par-4, namely in four shots, then this is classed as one under par; a five is level par. If you hit the green by mistake add a one-shot penalty to your score, if you have more than five shots then add the amount on top of the par plus-one i.e. six shots is one over on a par-4, seven shots is two over.

Record your score and make notes of what shots were played on each of the holes… and good luck with those "plus-one" birdies, you may find them a lot easier to find than the traditional birdies.

Par 4 hole

Plus-one is ideal for honing your "up-and-down" abilities.

Practice point

Golf is many things to many people but ultimately there is the element of competition, against the course, against others, and against yourself and your goals. When playing, in whatever situation, try to recreate something of the competition. Even if you are only playing for peanuts, or pride, take care. It doesn't matter if you don't succeed; it's still fun. But it's better to try hard than waste time on the course with careless shots and lack of concentration.

Tip

Plus-one will develop your confidence in getting up and down so always make sure you are playing approach shots within your limits; don't overreach at all.

Plan your practice

Practice should have a purpose, something to focus on; this is the same with playing. To keep your practice focused and relevant allow yourself to look forward to something different from the norm such as playing a new course or entering a competition.

Focus your attention on that. Then write down what you want to achieve. Build your practice around this goal for a week, a month, or a year, depending on how far away the event is. Practice aimed on this one goal will, of course, have benefits for your whole game. Rather than think in terms of just "practice," why not break it down into manageable parts. Think in terms of:
- pre-match
- straight between matches
- post-match.

Pre-match

Out of the car and first onto the 1st tee is unlikely to result in successful scoring. Consider preparing for competitions; there are multiple benefits. Physically, you should warm and stretch essential muscles and mobilize joints. Psychologically, you need to send messages to your body that a "performance" is required and establish "the zone" of concentration, essential in golf. Skills wise, pre-match preparation ensures success with all major shots required for your round, a confidence booster in itself.

Have a look at the ultimate pre-match ritual (right). This is probably more than you can manage but consider the breakdown of elements and create your own routine proportionally.

Ultimate pre-match practice

Phase One—The range
- five minutes stretching, particularly back and arms
- 56 degree sand wedge-shots—about 15 balls
- 5–10 balls with each 9 iron
  then 7 iron
  then 5 iron
  then 5 wood
  then driver
- 15–20 more sand wedge shots.
Throughout, concentrate on balance and smooth technique. Approximate time: 20 minutes

Phase Two—The chipping green
- 20 chip shots from 20 to 50 yards to specific targets.

Phase Three—The putting green
- hit 8–10 putts from 20 and 40 feet
- take the average miss from both, average those together
- make 10–20 putts in a row from that distance, usually around 30–40 inches.
This warm-up is extensive. It depends on having the time and facilities to complete it. As your standard improves and the competition gets fiercer, the opposition will invest more time in preparation; so must you too if you are to compete successfully.

Between matches

There are a few guidelines that can apply to all types of practice—whether on the range or on the course.

Do's and don'ts on the range include:

- when hitting range balls, quality of shot is essential, not the quantity; practice makes permanent
- start with the higher irons, work your way to the driver
- do not try to modify your swing on the range; correct swing faults with a lesson, then practise to embed improved technique
- use a consistent club to implement changes, possibly a 6 iron
- pre-shot routine practice is effective on the range; place the balls far enough away to encourage "fresh starts"
- simulate a few tough holes.

There are other considerations too. Work through the bag hitting different shots with each club—high fade, low fade, high draw, low draw. Also practise "non-full" shots such as punch shots and half shots. Discover how far you can hit short irons with three quarter and half swings. Use grass ranges if possible and play from poor lies; you won't be phased when you are in competition. Finally, practise into the wind as well as against it.

Short-game practice should remind you that the task is to get the ball into the hole. Chipping, bunker work, and putting practice is time well spent. Spend approximately 60 percent of available practice time in these areas to build confidence and shoot lower scores.

Try different approaches

- start close and work back to build confidence
- take one ball only and treat it as you would on the course: mark it, visualize the line, go through the pre-shot routine and chip/putt
- concentrate hard on short shots; chip uphill and downhill with various clubs
- try pitches, lobs, and flop shots from a variety of lies
- vary the length of bunker shots including those difficult 20-yard carries.

Post-match practice

Finally, how about post-competition practice routines? Top pros do not head for the bar after their round. They use the practice ground to work on aspects of their round which were below par. Technique is re-established and negative thoughts are dispelled and replaced by positive thinking and optimism about the next round.

Practice can be anywhere (almost) any time. Having a few practice balls in the home or workplace can be fun and invaluable. Hitting a couple of practice shots is also a good stress buster.

Course Management

It's simple. The aim of golf is to progress around the course from the first hole to the eighteenth, ensuring the ball leaves the tee and reaches the pin in the least number of shots. In order to achieve this... you must manage the course.

Think afresh...

The essence of course management is adopting a strategy for moving from point A to point B, from the tee to the green. Within the strategy you are aiming for minimal fuss, taking the least number of shots, managing all outside problems as and when they occur, with the utmost of care. When you're on top of your game, you will manage the course. When you're not playing well, the course will manage you.

Orienteering

For a moment it is worth considering how a non-golfer might approach the problem. If an orienteer, for example, was negotiating the ground from A to B what skills would he employ? He might:

- look afresh at every hole, assessing the lie of the land without pre-conceptions; this may sound simple but an orienteer will inevitably be presented with unfamiliar terrain so he will always think afresh
- ensure, at all times, he has a good idea of where he is in relation to the surrounding area and his intended objective; once he is on the move the perspective changes so what was valid from the map at the start might not be relevant now
- use any pre-planned route or map only as a guide; he will know that maps and route planners are only a starting point.

If we, as golfers, can learn from the above we should:

- think uniquely about each hole
- not stop thinking as we play the hole
- use course maps, and other advice, as a starting point only.

Avoid pre-conceptions

Added into information about the course is also knowledge of your own game. It is very easy for somebody to tell you how you play a golf hole but to do this they need to know your game extremely well. Probably they don't! Their advice may involve distances, club selections, or shots you haven't mastered or don't feel confident with.

Listen to advice—but make your own decisions. The next few pages (164–175) will provide a clear framework on which you can base your thinking and planning. You will be introduced to what may be, for you, some new ideas:

- reactive targeting
- attack points
- handrailing
- aiming off
- pacing
- course reviews.

remember... Damage limitation is an essential element of successful course management. If you are in trouble, concentrate on returning your ball to the fairway, giving yourself the opportunity to play a telling shot. Good for your morale and your score!

The course map

As golfers we cannot predict from a pre-analysis of a course map (sometimes called the "shot-saver") what is going to happen when out on the course. We can, however, use the course map as a basic guide with extra information being added from what we see "on the ground." So, always keep your eyes open.

In particular use the map to give you distances as a guide (also see pages 172–173). Remember that most course maps don't provide contours or elevation, which can be a key consideration when selecting a shot.

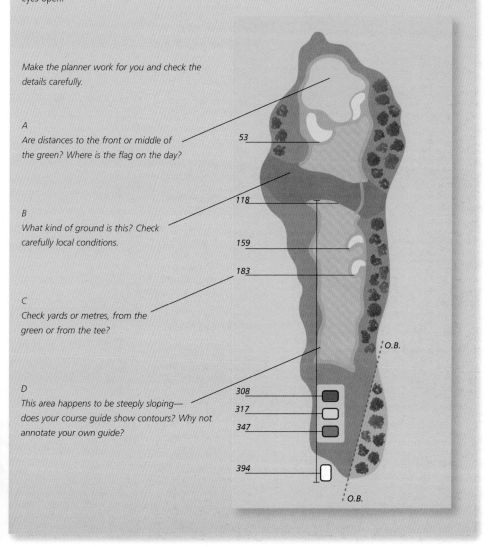

Make the planner work for you and check the details carefully.

A
Are distances to the front or middle of the green? Where is the flag on the day?

53

118

B
What kind of ground is this? Check carefully local conditions.

159

183

C
Check yards or metres, from the green or from the tee?

O.B.

D
This area happens to be steeply sloping— does your course guide show contours? Why not annotate your own guide?

308

317

347

394

O.B.

Reactive targeting

Reactive targeting is a twofold skill. It comprises the ability to recognize the potential risks that are presented to you when you stand over a shot, and then the identification, relative to those risks and your intended target, of the most suitable landing area.

Simple? Yes, and no. The process clarifies your thinking, allowing you to have a clear focus. As you stand over your shot, you know what you're aiming to do. But reaching that decision may not be easy. There are some important points to consider when selecting your reactive target.

Hazards and features

Be aware of the hazards and features close to your reactive target. Imagine a box surrounding your reactive target. This box should be reasonable in size, and in accordance with your ability. The box should have no hazards in it. Do not shrink this area to suit the hole—this box is designed around you, not the course. If you cannot find an area that is hazard free, then change your club and your approach until you can find the right area.

Ability level

Your reactive target should be relevant to your ability level. Professional golfers will not hit a shot they cannot hit successfully eight out of ten times. This allows them to approach every shot feeling relaxed and confident about what they are going to do. Consider the most appropriate golf club to use on your shot. Your reactive target shouldn't only be reachable with your very best shot, at the limit of a club. It should be achievable eight out of ten times.

Henrik Stenson of Sweden and caddie Fanny Suneson on the 2nd hole during the second round of the KLM Open. Fanny is one of a number of top caddies who players trust, and rely upon, for advice on strategy and club/shot slection.

remember... You must not let course management take your attention from other aspects of your game. Importantly, always commit to your shot once you have made a decision. Trying to steer the ball is never a good idea.

Your next shot

There is no point aiming at a reactive target that does not allow you to play your next shot. Our orienteer (see page 162) will not navigate towards a raging river and try and cross when there is a bridge further up that can be used. This may be a longer route but it is a route without risk that still allows him to cross. Always think, what will my next reactive target be?

Don't forget

- Be confident in your choice and consider all possible outcomes, adopting a clear focus on what your intended goal is.
- If you feel stretched, change your club, change your target. If you can play a shot that avoids risk, then there is no risk.
- Make your decision and fully commit to the shot that you want to hit. Make your target be your last thought as you start the golf swing.

Reactive targeting—an example

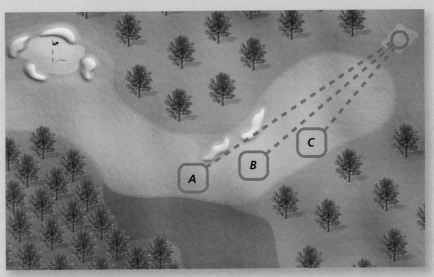

Reactive targeting is a balance between what you want to achieve, what risks you dare take... and what your game will allow you to do.
Shot **C** is the least risky and the easiest but it leaves problems of distance and line with the next shot.

A is clearly the best option but it is testing and demands a long drive. **B** is a good compromise but what is the state of the game or your score? Course management is all about making good choices.

know the language

Reactive targeting is assessing the options and choosing the best possible landing area for a golf shot.

Attack point

As we have seen on pages 164–165, you are looking for a target, the most suitable landing area in any given situation. It's rarely simply the pin. Similarly with playing shots in, you will not necessarily be looking to play the shot from as near to the target as possible. You need to identify your attack point, the best point from which to approach the green. This is a simple concept, but crucial when playing any golf hole. In real terms, this may mean laying down the driver and picking up a 5 iron. On the tee it might mean taking the shot from the edge of the box or two club lengths back from the tee. There is a link between the reactive target and the attack point; the first identifies the required landing area to ensure the ball comes to rest in the best possible spot to attack the green.

Making the decision

On page 162 we looked at how an orienteer might tackle a golf problem. With attack points we can make a comparison with a group of soldiers trying to mount an assault. For them the problem is twofold. They need all the possible information about the target—how far away, how well defended, elevation etc. They *also* need details of where they can attack from. It's the same with golf, although perhaps a little less important.

You will need to consider some of the following to find the best angle of attack to the green:

the target	the attack point
pin position	lie
protection	distance to target
elevation	line of sight
slope	hazards
hazards	

In some cases you may even have to consider wind direction. One attack point may put you into the full force of the wind, another may allow you gain some shelter or come in from a slightly different angle where the wind may aid the shape of your shot.

Know your game

Just as with determining your reactive target, it is vitally important you know your own game. You can't rely on hitting the perfect shot every time but you will know what shots give you a greater likelihood of success. Knowing your own strengths and limitations is essential. If you are simply not capable of playing a draw at the moment, a percentage shot to the right side of the fairway on a left hand dogleg will be the percentage shot. If 80 yard pitches are a strength, then go for the pin from a good position on the fairway. Don't forget; all of these shots can be practised. Head for the practice ground and improve your game.

Think back to front

When assessing your strategy to reach the hole it is often easier to review your potential options in the reverse, i.e. looking first at the green and thinking back from here to the tee. Use this technique when you have difficult decisions to make. Shots can look very different viewed in this way.

Choose each attack point with care, as this should determine how you play each hole... and how well you score.

know the language

Your attack point is the best position from which to reach your target.

Attack point—an example

As an example, let's look at a par five with an elevated green that slopes from left to right. You have hit your drive to **C**. In this case, the best direction to come in from will be right of the fairway, point **A**. This will present you with a wider green to approach, and will allow you to have a better view of the flag position. This means that if you push or pull the ball the likelihood of it missing the green is dramatically reduced.

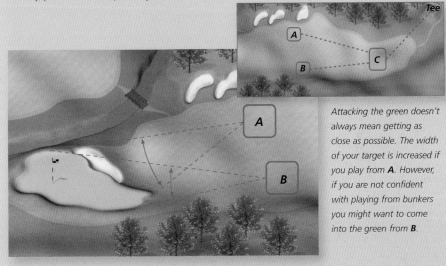

*Attacking the green doesn't always mean getting as close as possible. The width of your target is increased if you play from **A**. However, if you are not confident with playing from bunkers you might want to come into the green from **B**.*

remember... When planning your shot, don't forget that the target and where you land the ball will not be the same. Your attack point is where you want the ball to be positioned. To reach this point you will need to allow for roll, backspin, slope, etc.

Handrailing

Handrailing is something you may well do without thinking... but if you can build it into your game consciously then you have an extra tool in your bag. Handrailing means sending the ball on a path, inside of, and parallel to, that of a feature such as a fence, line of trees, course markers or contours. Once you send the ball on your intended course of travel to follow a handrail, you figuratively 'hold on to it' all the way towards your target.

Why handrailing?

Determining reactive targets and attack points are all fairly simple concepts—with obvious advantages. Handrailing has to be considered more carefully, although the opportunities to use it are commonplace. Most courses and many holes have features running along-side fairways.

First you must determine your target. Then look at the features lining the fairway. Do they follow the line of your shot—or, more importantly, could your shot follow the line of

know the language

Handrailing is using a feature that lines a hole as a guide to your shot.

Handrailing—an example

If a hole was to bend to the left, your intended ball flight should handrail the left side of the hole for two reasons—the first reason being that you end up closer to your target (green), and the second reason being that by playing up the left side you will have more space ahead of you.

If you decide to use handrailing from the tee always use the full width of the teeing area to facilitate the shot you want to play.

the feature? If the two match up then you can envisage your shot, handrailing along the feature. There is the important visual element, allowing you to "see" a shot and, as the example shows, a "handrailed" shot can put you closer to the green and give you more room to play with when playing a dogleg. But there are two points of which to be aware.

● Make sure you can achieve the shot. Don't play it too fine. Frequently the handrails will be problems (trees, out-of-bounds markers, the edge of a lake) so give yourself a little room for error. Widen your intended course of travel away from what you are handrailing, there is no need to be glued to the feature you are hitting the ball along.

● If you are handrailing from the tee, always hit from the most advantageous position on the tee box; this doesn't have to be the middle of the box.

Handrailing contours

Handrailing can also be applied to following the slope on the course. If presented with, for example, a tee shot, and you have a fairway that slopes from right to left, it would make sense to send the ball along the high side, i.e. the right. This would allow the ball to gain more distance because of the lie of the land.

Working along the contours is also good for visualizing the shot.

remember... When following this, or any, technique, always look at the benefits versus the risk before you make your commitment to the shot. Don't let your eagerness to use a new technique override your regular golf brain.

Aiming off

Aiming off refers to avoiding a fixed hazard, by shaping or moving the ball away from that hazard en route to your intended target or attack point. It is not the same as what we might call "aiming away." Aiming away implies a straight shot, used to go past a hazard. Neither is it "aiming over" where we are simply taking a hazard out by flying over it. Aiming off means shaping your shot so, although you still have a clear target, the ball always moves away from, not just past and not across, the hazard.

Stacy Lewis hits her approach shot on the 18th hole as her father/caddie Dale looks on during the third round of The US Women's Open. The hazards, water and trap, will influence her shot.

The advantages

Reaching your target can be difficult when you have hazards in the way. Say you have a target behind a bunker. Is it better to aim direct, or fade or draw a ball into the target? By going direct you have two problems: perfecting the distance beyond the bunker (particularly if you need to pull the ball up short) and taking on the bunker itself. You add in a risk element. By trying to use a shape of shot to bring you into the flag you will also be adding risk; if you come up short you'll be in the hazard. Aiming off means that the ball will be falling away from the hazard as it comes to a stop.

The key to aiming off is that the technique allows you to make errors of shot with no serious consequence.

Aiming off as a starting point

Look at the problem in front of you. If you think aiming off will give the best balance of achievability and safety then it is the shot for you. The main problem is likely to be your inability to play the shot. (In truth your main problem may be not believing you can make the shot!) If you do lack the technique, or confidence, the next best policy is attempt any shot that doesn't require aiming straight at the hazard.

know the language

Aiming off is avoiding hazards by shaping shots away from that hazard.

Aiming off—an example

From the attack point we need to start the ball at the target and let it gently fade away from the hazard (option **C**). This uses the principle of aiming off, producing a percentage shot allowing the player to avoid the main hazard, the left hand bunker, and access a large area of the green. It requires an ability to shape a shot. For the player able to draw the ball option **B** is worth considering. Initially the ball is taken away from the hazard but there is more risk as the ball nears the green. For players unable to shape a shot option **A** is a possibility. Errors in clubbing or the quality of the strike will likely leave the player bunkered. If your natural shot is straight you could aim for the heart of the green right of the bunker. Back to the principle however. Aiming off is all about playing the ball in such a way as to move it away from the hazard to the target area or attack point.

Aiming off is a decision making issue—weighing up your options and abilities

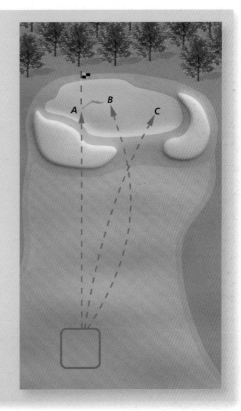

remember... More than any other course management technique, aiming off requires the ability to shape shots. Don't attempt the shot unless you can play it—but if you can't play it, don't give up on aiming off. Go to the practice ground and perfect your fade and draw.

Distance awareness

Knowing where you are on a golf hole is vital. How many yards (or metres) it is to your target is key information when choosing your club. You cannot manage the course or your round without this information, all the way from a tee on a 580-yard par 5 up to the 60- 70-yards shots into the green.

Tiger makes good use of his course planner that he and his caddie will have heavily annotated.

Learning pacing

This may sound obvious but many players do make errors. There are two approaches.

Natural paces

You can establish how many natural paces it takes you to cover 10, 20, 30 and 50 yards with and without a golf bag. This requires a little practice and, if you are really serious about it, you should measure yourself on a known 100 yard stretch of ground before coming to the course. You can use running

know the language

Distance awareness is knowing exactly where you are on a golf hole.

tracks but remember these are normally 100 metres and some math will be needed to calculate your yardage.

Yard paces

You can train yourself to step at yard paces when counting distances, again with or without a bag. This may be the simpler method once you've learned it as you won't need to do any math in your head when you're on the course.

With both techniques you will need some means of keeping track of how many paces have been counted. With the use of a clicker you will be able to still engage in conversation while counting paces, allowing for a more social round of golf or concentration on other aspects of your game. With practice, pacing can be reasonably accurate, provided the pacing is kept relatively short. Assuming there are course markings, there should be no reason for measuring distances above 150 yards, maybe even 100 yards.

Steep uphill sections will considerably shorten the length of paces, as may awkward terrain such as areas of rough. Unfortunately there is no rule on assessing this, only personal judgement and practice. The steeper the uphill slope, the shorter the steps.

know the language
Pacing out is simply the process of working out distances on foot.

Using the course markings
When assessing the distance from A to B, be aware of distance being increased when looking at an uphill shot, and vice versa with a downhill shot.

Club distance
Knowing distances on the course is only the start of the process. You must know how far you hit each club. The best way is to go to a range where you can ask the local professional to use a yard stick or a range finder to assess each club within your bag.

It is a good idea to have a system which tells the professional when you have hit a bad shot, so that it is not counted and, of course, when you are to move onto the next club. Try to start with the wedges, as this will help with the communication with the professional while you get into a routine. Five good shots with each club are usually sufficient, then move on to the next club. Calculate the total of the five shots and divide by five for your average distance.

Club 7	Distance
Shot 1	150 yards
Shot 2	152 yards
Shot 3	157 yards
Shot 4	157 yards
Shot 5	155 yards
Total	771 yards
Divided by 5	154.2 yards

Once you have assessed your clubs you should be able to plan your bag. However, if you notice that there is a big gap in distance between your irons i.e. the 7 iron goes 20 yards further than your 8 iron, or two clubs hit almost the same distance, then you have a fault common to many golfers —your shafts do not match. This could be the shaft orientation or the kick points are different from one to the next. It may be just psychological but first consider the shafts are not right (see page 135).

Alternatively you may have a hybrid that travels the distance you require. Whatever you do, keep the club you are most comfortable playing.

Yards or metres
Most courses in the UK and USA use yards as standard measurements, but be aware that courses in Europe and the Far East tend to use metres. Check it out when you get to the course. As a simple rule of thumb, to convert from metres to yards, it's about 10% off. Or you can remember a few key measurements:

20 metres = 21.8 yards
50 metres = 54.6 yards
80 metres = 87.5 yards

remember... Be aware:
- are there markers on the course (posts, plates etc.)
- at what distances as they placed (100, 150 etc.)
- what units are they using (yards, metres)
- where are they marked from (front or middle of the green)
- where is the flag (front, middle or back of the green)?

Course review

Course review **is a twofold concept. First it requires an**
assessment of each golf hole played. Second, and equally important,
it implies the retrospective lessons that can be learnt through a form
of analysis. Play your round, keep careful notes and learn from the
results. There are two documents required for good course reviews:
your full scorecard and your course planner.

Par 3

Hole	Shots	Target hit	Inside 50 yards	Inside 20 yards	Greenside bunker	Shots to green	Putts	Notes
		Yes/No	Yes/No	Yes/No	Yes/No			
		Choice	Inside 2 yards	Inside 2 yards	Inside 2 yards			
		Good/Bad	Yes/No	Yes/No	Yes/No			

Par 4

Hole	Shots	Target (1) hit	Target (2) hit	Inside 50 yards	Inside 20 yards	Greenside bunker	Shots to green	Putts	Notes
		Yes/No	Yes/No	Yes/No	Yes/No				
		Choice	Inside 2 yards	Inside 2 yards	Inside 2 yards				
		Good/Bad	Yes/No	Yes/No	Yes/No				

Par 5

Hole	Shots	Target (1) hit	Target (2) hit	Target (3) yards	Inside 50 yards	Inside 20	Greenside	Shots bunker	Putts to green	Notes
		Yes/No	Yes/No	Yes/No	Yes/No	Yes/No	Yes/No			
		Choice	Choice	Choice	Inside 2 yards	Inside 2 yards	Inside 2 yards			
		Good/Bad	Good/Bad	Good/Bad	Yes/No	Yes/No	Yes/No			

Your annotated scorecard will need variations for par 3, 4, and 5 holes.

Scorecard and stat building

By keeping an annotated scorecard you can analyse the round and see where work is most needed.

These are simplified versions of what you can use to suit your own game. In each case there is allowance for an extra shot to the green. Note that the Choice and Notes columns allow you to be subjective too.

There are some points you might like to think about or add when scoring:

1   The target is your reactive target but don't forget that, ideally on a par 4, and certainly a par 5, your target may also be your attack point.

2   You may like to add extra notes for: the length of putts (how close you put long putts for example, how many short putts you sank etc.), fairway bunkers, fairways hit (although, of course, most of your targets will be fairways) etc.

3   Club selection can also be noted but remember that this will be relative to weather conditions.

The key with stat building is just that—to keep building until pictures emerge of where you are strong and where you may need to practise more, or better.

Annotated course guide

With your course guide you can look at each hole and see how different approaches and better shots might help you score less next time out.

On holes where you noted particular difficulties, mark out the best route (based on your own skill and limitations) from tee to green. Then mark what you actually played for and achieved. Would you now plan, and play your attack points and reactive targeting differently? Did your handrailing and aiming off work?

Often the best way to learn is through making mistakes… and being able to store this information. When you've decided to log some holes, stick with it. Don't just ignore the very bad holes. You won't learn much from just the holes where you played well. And keep records over time; it's only through accumulating evidence that you can see patterns of success, and failings, develop.

know the language
Course review is learning from statistical and objective records of your golf.

remember... It's what is written
on the scorecard that counts. You may think you play some holes better than others, and are more adept at some shots than others, but statistical evidence will show whether this is true or not. Do trust the stats and work hard on where your weaknesses lie.

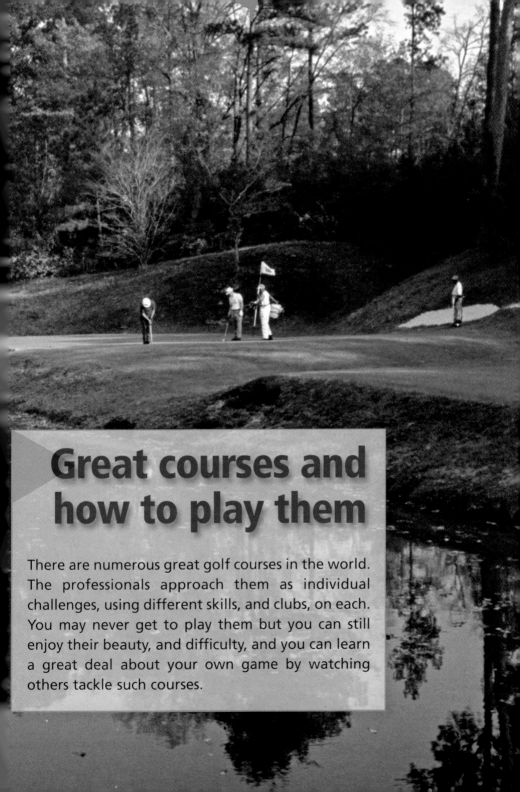

Great courses and how to play them

There are numerous great golf courses in the world. The professionals approach them as individual challenges, using different skills, and clubs, on each. You may never get to play them but you can still enjoy their beauty, and difficulty, and you can learn a great deal about your own game by watching others tackle such courses.

Augusta National

Perhaps with the exception of the Old Course at St Andrews, the Augusta National course in Georgia, home of The Masters, is the most famous in the world. In terms of sculptured beauty and manicured greens there is probably no course to rival it.

factfile
- CREATED **1933**
- LOCATION **Georgia, USA**
- DISTANCE **7,290 yards**
- PAR **72**

The formation of the Club was spearheaded by Bobby Jones—Amateur Open champion of both the US and Great Britain in 1930. He retired from competition play soon after his joint triumph and joined up with a golfing friend, Clifford Roberts, and a Scottish designer, Dr. Alister MacKenzie, to create a course that was both a challenge to the top players and a pleasure for average club golfers.

To achieve the latter ambition the fairways were wide, there was very little rough, and few fairway bunkers. Even hapless amateurs had a good chance of approaching the green.

Defending the course

The "defence" for the course, against the long and accurate hitting of professionals, was found in the greens. These were, and are, large, heavily contoured, and extremely fast. The challenge for any type of player is to get on to the green into such a position that a two-putt is a possibility. There are few tap-ins for the top players and numerous examples of four- or five-putts even in The Masters.

It is hard to separate the course from the competition but the Augusta National does have a life beyond The Masters. The early membership was drawn from friends of Jones and people like him. This set the trend for a club with a membership still made up of rich and influential people (not all of whom are great golfers!). It's not a course on which you can just book a tee-time.

Prayers... and the future

One of Augusta's greatest challenges is the famous Amen Corner (players need to offer up a prayer). Its three holes—11, 12 and 13—all feature hard-to-hit greens where water and bunkers play havoc with confidence.

The course is under constant scrutiny and, like many other championship courses, has been changed to take account of new technologies and longer hitting. Whatever happens, the club's management are acutely aware of their course's place in golf heritage.

Robert Tyre Jones

Players who become course architects will often build courses that mirror their defining skill or skills. Bobby Jones was one of the great putters of his time, which can only explain the very large greens at Augusta National. He was integral to the design there and also to the set-up of The Masters, played at Augusta since 1934. Bobby Jones was a perfectionist, spending endless hours calculating and hitting experimental shots from a range of angles in order to achieve the desired result. He continued to make small changes and adjustments every year. This continues today, allowing the course to evolve with the requirements of the modern game.

What you need...

Because of the incredible speed of the greens the only way to gain control of shots is to play the slopes. This will allow you to stop the ball quicker than you could playing with, or along, the contours of the green. On Augusta National, therefore, you need to understand which way the green slopes and what is the best possible attack point. With any elevated green you will be less likely to see the pin position, take the time to have a look. On other greens you need to check the contours beforehand if possible.

You won't always have a choice but where possible, fire into the slope, not from an angle.

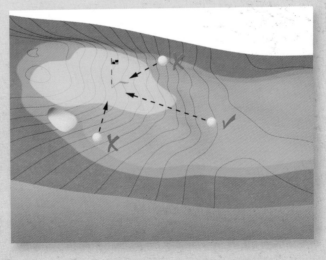

Gleneagles

Gleneagles is situated on its own estate in the Perthshire moorland amongst a landscape of spectacular rock-faced peaks (the Trossachs and Grampians), and is famed for its spectacular scenery. It is easy to see why any golfer would go out of their way to enjoy the splendid landscape and the challenges that Gleneagles has to offer.

factfile
- CREATED **1919**
- LOCATION **Scotland**
- DISTANCE **6,471 yards**
- PAR **70**

Gleneagles today boasts three championship courses, the King's, Queen's and PGA Centenary course (where the 40th Ryder Cup is scheduled to be played in 2014), and the Wee course (nine holes), and is considered to be one of Scotland's most luxurious golf resorts.

The King's course (18 holes) and Queen's course (originally 9 holes) are the work of James Braid (1870–1950), winner of five British Opens at the turn of the nineteenth century. These splendid courses, which were opened one year before the hotel in 1919, were designed to test the most skilled of golfers while still giving pleasure to the visiting guests of the famous hotel. The PGA Centenary course, at 7,088 yards, is the longest inland course in Scotland, and was designed by Jack Nicklaus in 1993.

Spirit of the course

Gleneagles' King's course is as famous for being Scottish as it is for being a world-ranked golf course. It sums up the spirit of Scotland and indeed the spirit of golf. Each hole has been given a Gaelic name reflecting its character. For example, the 178-yard 5th hole, "Het Girdle" (Hot Pan), consists of an exposed high plateau green, surrounded by deep green side bunkers, where the only sanctuary can be found on the green. The 17th hole, "Warslin Lea" (Wrestling Ground), reflects the problems many golfers have negotiating this long, sweeping par 4.

James Braid

To play the King's course well you need to understand the genius of its architect, James Braid, who created deceptive and challenging greens. It's unlikely that you will have the luxury of time assessing the greens before competition play, but you can still help yourself when approaching new greens.

First look at the contours of the surrounding land. Understand which way it lies to appreciate the slopes of the green itself. Only when you are clear about the overall slope of the green should you start looking at smaller undulations within it. Always view from the lowest point and then from behind the ball. Walk beside the line that you hope the ball will travel to try to feel with your feet how the ball will roll.

What you need...

In order for you to understand the geniuse of James Braid's work you should take time to explore the greens he has designed. The great views Mr Braid was always able to capture when designing a course should be a clue to you. You need to first look at the contours of the surrounding ground before making any assessment of the greens, ask which way the surrounding area falls, then use this information to challenge the slopes of the green itself.

As you walk downhill to a green it may look as if the green is uphill. This is often an optical illusion. Check from side-on and place the green in it's overall context. In **A** the green may look uphill but is flat. In **B** it may look flat but slopes away from you.

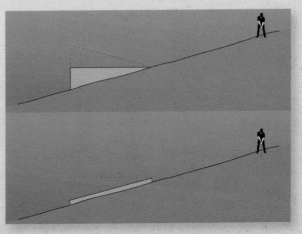

Les Bordes

Les Bordes in the Loire valley is possibly the most challenging golf course in Europe. There are very few par-72 courses today where the course record is only one under par (by Jean Van de Velde). In fact, if you break 80 off the back tees, you will be rewarded with permanent recognition—your name, golf club, and national flag being included on the club's honour role board next to other amateurs and professionals who have achieved this feat.

factfile
- CREATED **1986**
- LOCATION **France**
- DISTANCE **7,024 yds**
- PAR **72**

This exceptional course was created for the owner Baron Marcel Bich (the man behind Bic pens and owner of the Les Bordes Estate) and his friend the entrepreneur Yoshiaki Sakurai as a place to invite friends and for their own personal pleasure. The course was designed by Texan Robert von Hagge, who has been credited with the creation or redesign of more than 250 golf courses worldwide.

Course design

At Les Bordes great care was taken to blend in and sweep this course around the beautiful mature forest of oak, fir, and birch trees, the reflections of which can be seen in the many lakes around the course. Water comes into play on at least 12 of the holes, and this feature, combined with island greens, massive bunkers, elevated fairways, and a monster length of 7,024 yards off the back tees, creates a challenging masterpiece for even the most experienced player.

Practice makes perfect

Practice facilities are best described as an experience of golfing fore-play creating the anticipation of what is to come, with a magnificent driving range that is pleasing to the eye and a large grass tee from which to play your shots. There is also one of the largest practice greens in Europe, stretching over 3,500 square yards, situated behind the elegant club house.

Les Bordes offers all the golfing challenges, and will for many years to come be the one course that can stand on its own as a golf club where any person can record their name for posterity—if they are up to the challenge!

Robert von Hagge

It is not difficult to see Robert von Hagge's influences as he was simply born into his trade. His father, Ben F. von Hagge, managed and designed many golf courses in and around the Chicago area. Before he was even 17, Robert had experienced most aspects of the golf course, from grounds maintenance to caddying to golf tuition. Having graduated from Purdue University Agriculture School, majoring in landscape architecture, he secured an apprenticeship with Dick Wilson, one of America's foremost golf course architects. Within four years, Robert was recognized as a principal architect within his profession and he went on to start his own design firm in 1962. To date, Robert von Hagge has created some of the world's most outstanding and award-winning courses, and has been responsible for the design, redesign or partial design of over 250 golf courses in the US, Caribbean, and 16 other countries.

What you need...

This is one of the toughest golf courses in the world today. When playing a difficult course, you need to prepare. One technique is to plan in terms of "Maslow's Hierarchy of Needs." Stripped to the bare bones, this is a pyramid you climb to reach the top. You can see how it applies to golf... something like this will help you achieve your goals (or even a score of 80 at Les Bordes).

Self-actualization
(realizing full potential)
- The goal—achieved by progressing through the previous steps.

Esteem
(achievement through respect and competence)
- Set mini goals and enjoy a sense of achievement when you reach them.

Social
(acceptance and belonging)
- When in a group playing golf you are more comfortable in a group that accepts you being there... it's where you belong.

Safety
(comfortable in own environment)
- If you enjoy where you are and feel you have everything you need then there is no reason for anything to go wrong.

Basic
(food and water)
- A good nutritional intake to last the round will allow you to feel confident.

Muirfield Village

Muirfield Village, situated just to the north of Columbus, Ohio, covers an area of 220 acres and is home to two golf courses and a luxurious golf village, all of which attract the rich and famous to Muirfield's neighbourhood. Opened in 1974 it is considered one of America's top 25 courses, and represents the modern-day course specifically created for spectacular televised events.

factfile
- CREATED **1974**
- LOCATION **Ohio, USA**
- DISTANCE **7,221 yards**
- PAR **72**

Designed for spectating and playing

The course, designed by Jack Nicklaus in association with Desmond Muirhead, is at Muirfield Village Golf Club. Nicklaus created Muirfield Village as a self-sustaining and self-sufficient "principality," functioning to raise money for street lighting and the like through its powers for tax collection and the establishment of its own neighborhood council.

Ideals

The course was designed both for spectators and for the enjoyment of golfers of any standard. In the words of Jack Nicklaus: "I set out to build not only an outstanding golf course for every level of player, but a magnificent course for watching a tournament... I thought The Masters was a great thing for golf and that I'd like to do the same thing in Columbus." Spectators are therefore catered for at every stage of the course, with specially prepared vantage points created for the absolute viewing experience.

Each year, changes and alterations are made to the course to accommodate developments in the game and to increase the experience for both members and spectators. An example of this would be the recent lengthening of several holes to increase the challenge for the "big hitters." Other changes have reduced incidents of spectator congestion. The course can be reconfigured through the use of a variety of teeing grounds to facilitate everyday play by its members.

From the golfer's point of view one particular characteristic of Muirfield Village is that there are frequent "blind" areas on the fairways. Therefore it is necessary to use the yardage book to locate hazards such as bunkers, or more importantly streams, that run across the fairways.

Major tournaments

Muirfield Village is the host to the Memorial Tournament, an annual event held on Memorial Day weekend. The Memorial Tournament has grown into one of golf's premier events, and is often referred to as the "fifth Major." Muirfield Village has also seen The US Amateur (junior and senior), the Ryder Cup, and the Solheim Cup grace its greens.

Jack Nicklaus

Nicklaus is considered one of the best players in golfing history. His talent however has no boundaries and transcends effortlessly into one of golf course design of supreme standing. His experience in design has extended over three decades during which he has built up a formidable team, Nicklaus Design, and they have gone a long way to challenge and elevate the standards of golf course architecture.

His course designs account for every aspect of the game, recognizing the evolution of golf into one of the most popular sports. Nicklaus seemingly sees nothing as insurmountable and is able to create elegant courses which are a challenge for all.

What you need...

Muirfield Village is typical of many courses that you might play where there are blind areas on the fairway.

When approaching a shot you need an overview of the hazards that face you. Bunkers, trees, water hazards... you need to know both where, and how far away, these features are. This is where your course guide or shot saver will be invaluable.

When using your guide it's a good tip to orientate to the ground, not the direction you're facing. Simply turn the guide in your hands so it is aligned to the

Once you have orientated your guide keep it aligned for an accurate assessment of direction and distance.

ground. Once orientated, you should be able to gain a clear picture of the hole and know where everything is. What this means is that you should be able to imagine a straight line from you, through where you are on the book to the feature on the book, and then to that same feature on the ground, in one continuous straight line. This sets the book in relation to the ground. Once this is established you should be able to relate what you see on the page to what is in front of you. This is only a gauge but it should give you a good idea of what and where these hidden hazards are.

Pebble Beach

Pebble Beach, located in Monterey County, California is famed for its coastal beauty and celebrity residents. It is also home to the world-famous Pebble Beach Golf Links, rated the top public course in the US. Its holes create spectacular views over the Pacific ocean and are set amongst established trees, including the Lone Cypress, the symbol for Pebble Beach.

> **fact**file
> - CREATED **1918**
> - LOCATION **California, USA**
> - DISTANCE **7,024 yards**
> - PAR **72**

In 1918 Sam Morse, a property developer, commissioned Jack Neville to design a links golf course on a prime piece of golfing real estate on this spectacular peninsula. This Neville did, creating a masterpiece of breathtaking beauty.

Layout

Pebble Beach is an out-and-back layout with the 11th hole found at the end of the course. With the course exposed to the Californian Pacific coast, the wind will often be a dominating feature, which during a round will naturally not always be from the same direction! Because of this, the golfer will require knowledge of a wide array of shots.

The course starts comparatively gently, with the cliff edges posing the threat. On many holes, golfers are required to strike their ball from elevated tees into a background filled by the often violent Pacific Ocean. Strong gusts of wind and the tight lines required to reach safety also make good scoring tough work. The 7th hole is short (only 120 yards long) and the green small. Add in the wind factor from the Pacific and you have your own little nightmare. The sequence of shots required over the 8th, 9th, and 10th holes results in possibly the toughest par 4s in the world—the result of a competition is often decided just on how these holes are played.

Design changes

Pebble Beach has hosted The US Amateur Championship (first played here in 1929), and the four-round National Pro-Am is played each February (formerly the Bing Crosby National Pro-Am). Pebble Beach Golf Links has also been the venue for The US Open Championship, which is set to be here again in 2010.

Very few changes have been made to the original design. The course was remodeled by Henry Chandler Egan ahead of the 1929 US Amateur Championship, but the most recent change came in 1998 when the sale of a parcel of land forced changes to the 5th and 6th tees. Nicklaus became the architect for the changes and created a breathtaking par 3. The fact that no one has made any efforts to alter the design significantly since the course's inception, despite changes to technology and the game, is testament to Neville's vision.

Jack Neville

Not only was Jack Neville a real estate salesman but he was also an accomplished amateur golfer having won the California State Amateur Championships on seven occasions, the final two being played on his own creation at Pebble Beach Golf Links in 1922 and 1929. His vision for the course was taken from the natural beauty of the area, clearing very little to make way for the course. Neville created a figure-of-eight layout to accommodate as many holes as possible amongst the rocky Monterey coastline.

What you need...

Pebble Beach is exposed to the Pacific Ocean and, like most coastal courses, can "enjoy" strong winds. When playing into the wind you can try a number of techniques for better control. Overall you are aiming to swing softer—but with a longer club. Try the following:

- reduce club-head speed which, in turn, reduces ball backspin
- reduce your active wrists in the swing to bring the ball spin down
- grip down to make the shaft stiffer, again reducing the spin on the ball.

Using some or all of these techniques will give you far better control into wind rather than the ball ballooning up against the wind. Also the ball will roll further on landing, making up for the distance lost in flight.

Downwind your shots should be played as normal making sure to use less club because of the extra distance that can be gained playing with the wind. When dealing with a crosswind you could hit into the direction of the crosswind and let the wind naturally bring the ball back onto targets. Trying to shape shots in a strong wind can be dangerous as the wind will overemphasize any overcooked draw or fade.

Gripping down allows you to feel more in control.

Pine Valley

Pine Valley, New Jersey, certainly ranks as one of the world's finest courses. It has hosted the Walker Cup on two occasions (1935 and 1985), but its design has recently been compromised in order to accommodate spectators.

factfile
- CREATED **1913**
- LOCATION **New Jersey, USA**
- DISTANCE **6,999 yards**
- PAR **70**

The course was the brainchild of George Crump who is considered to have been the architect of one of the world's most punishing courses. His vision was to create a course on which a player is forced to use every club in the bag at some stage in the game.

Design

Pine Valley is said to have the finest collection of holes found on any one golf course. Each hole is of equal merit but for diverse reasons, requiring different technical approaches. The intensity of the course never wavers at a "lesser" hole.

Crump's design is such that no more than two holes are played in the same direction. In 1909 when Crump first saw the plot of land, it was a windswept area of sand dunes and scrub. Since then, much tree planting has taken place, and at no time does a player now see any hole other than the one they are playing. A player must hop from one green space to the next, negotiating water and bunker threats along the way; one mistake and the hole is lost.

Longings

Pine Valley can be used only by members and, because of this, few get the chance to play or experience this spectacular course. This is unfortunate, because Crump built a layout rife with strategic options that make it as fascinating to play the 100th time as it is to play the first time. And given the heroic scale of the natural features and how they were incorporated into the designs, nature steals the show and makes all but a handful of other courses and their hazards seem puny and almost irrelevant.

George Crump

George Arthur Crump was born in Philadelphia in 1871 and his career masterpiece at Pine Valley was created in golf's golden age in the early 1900s. He is one of few architects of his eminence who has no standing as a professional or amateur golfer; he merely had a passion for the game. Although Pine Valley is undoubtedly down to the genius of Crump, influences have also come from many great architects of the time, including Harry Colt who was noted for his creation of technical courses. This may have been why Crump targeted Colt to partner him in the creation of Pine Valley.

Unfortunately, Crump did not see his vision through to the end. He committed suicide on 24th January 1918, before the final four holes had been completed, leaving Colt to finish his ideas for Pine Valley.

What you need...

On long and difficult courses such as Pine Valley you are going to be faced with the widest range of yardages. Courses like these cannot be reduced to driver and wedge, so it is vital to have a balanced set of clubs. You will know when your clubs are not balanced when either you seem to hit two different clubs the same distance, or the gap between two "adjoining" clubs is massively different. Your swing should be effortless and constant, regardless of what club you hit, and should not change to accommodate different distances—except with the touch shots close to the green.

The problem of unbalanced clubs is increased if you use a mixture of woods, irons, and hybrids which may well overlap.

Robert Karlsson of Sweden looks over a shot with his caddie Gareth Lord on the 15th green during the final round of The US Open.

Royal Melbourne

Royal Melbourne Golf Club is located in the renowned
Melbourne sandbelt and boasts two world-class courses (the East
Course and West Course). It is considered to be the most prestigious
and indeed the oldest golf club in Australia.

▶ **fact**file
- CREATED **1926**
- LOCATION **Australia**
- DISTANCE **6,589 yards**
- PAR **72**

Although the Club was founded in 1891, Royal Melbourne became the course we know today only in the early 1930s, when Dr. Alister MacKenzie (the West Course architect) and Alex Russell (the East Course architect) completed their designs, with the assistance of the head greenkeeper Mick Morcom. The two courses are of tournament caliber and a combination of the best holes on each course (12 from the West and 6 from the East) creates the "tournament course," which was first used in 1959. This Composite course is only played during international golf tournaments. The Royal Melbourne was selected by the PGA as the first club outside the US to host the President's Cup and is due to host this tournament again in 2011.

MacKenzie's courses blend a balance between risk and reward. Like most notable course designers, both classic and modern, MacKenzie saw the value of creating a course that could be enjoyed by golfers of all levels.

The West Course opens with an instantly recognisable hole, as Mackenzie created a near mirror image of the 1st hole at the Old Course, St Andrews, Scotland. The 10th is a classic hole, with MacKenzie's handprint firmly left for posterity, being a par 4 of no more than 300 yards but with a vast dogleg and bunkers defending the angle. The last hole, however, a par 4 of 433 yards with a vicious dogleg to the right, is the pièce de résistance. MacKenzie was able to create a blind tee shot over a slope laden with bunkers, or rather a bunker made into a slope!

The future

The Royal Melbourne Club celebrated its centenary in 1991, and with the quality and challenge of its two major courses it should continue and prosper for many years to come.

Dr. Alister MacKenzie

MacKenzie was born in Wakefield, Yorkshire, UK in 1870. He initially trained as a doctor, but his career path soon changed and he entered the world of golf course design. Despite his obvious talent for design, MacKenzie was not a particularly good golfer. He took his inspiration from the land itself, seeing nature as the actual architect of a great course. In 1920 MacKenzie emigrated to the US where his most noted work was completed. He was one of the most celebrated course architects of the time, having had a hand in the design of Augusta National, Cypress Point, and Royal Troon. He was also commissioned to design the West Course at Royal Melbourne and went into partnership with Alex Russell, an Australian Open champion, to complete the East Course.

What you need...

When travelling to hot environments and doing any activity like golf where you are exposed to hot temperatures for long periods of time it is important to keep drinking water.

Isotonic drinks will also assist with hydration, and are best used during and after an event to help with performance. They will also supply your body with small quantities of carbohydrates for extra energy during the day. Try taking isotonic drinks with you onto the course.

Sun City

Sun City Resort—the creation of Gary Player and Ronald Kirby is located in Player's homeland, South Africa. Sun City has spectacular scenery and stretches over a tremendous expanse and contains two of the world's longest golf courses—the Gary Player Country Club course and The Lost City Golf Club.

▶ **fact**file
- CREATED **1970**
- LOCATION **South Africa**
- DISTANCE **6,938 yards**
- PAR **72**

These two courses developed by Gary Player demonstrate his respect for the environment and his wish to leave the land enhanced by his designs. Great care has been taken to work with the natural landscape and protect the local ecosystems.

The spectacular views and the presence of the wildlife make these courses the most scenic and interesting courses in Africa, let alone the world.

The Gary Player Country Club course is fairly flat, but the many water hazards, cunningly sited bunkers and hidden pin placements on the super-slick greens make up for the lack of gradient.

It has hosted the annual "Million Dollar Challenge" each December since 1981. The million dollar check has been the appeal for many world-class golfers who have graced these greens.

Lost City

The Lost City Golf Club is situated just over the hill from the Gary Player Country Club and, although both courses have similar characteristics, the Lost City Golf Club has a different layout. The front nine is desert style with undulating rocky terrain and large bunkers, whereas the back nine is more of a golf safari, with simply a fence separating the course from the Pilanesberg Game Reserve. There are views of the bushveld and mountainous terrain from this course, plus occasional glimpses of wildlife, sometimes even giraffes, from the back nine.

The most uncompromising hole is the par 3 13th. From the elevated tee, the view is of a clover-shaped green, surrounded by nine bunkers and a real water hazard—home to 40 Nile crocodiles—a ball in the water here is best forgotten!

The golf course covers more than 250 acres and incorporates 33,500 square yards of water features. For this reason (and the occurrence of wildlife, including spitting cobras), not surprisingly, golf carts are compulsory.

Gary Player

Gary Player is arguably one of the world's greatest golfers but his talent does not end there. Player has turned his attention to a number of off-course projects including his leading golf course design, marketing, and real-estate planning businesses. His team have been responsible for the design of several hundred golf courses stretching across the world.

Real thought goes into creating a golf course that will satisfy the most talented of players to the occassional golfer. Player's courses are flexible because they incorporate multiple tee positions and varying approaches.

What you need...

With any course like Sun City, you should follow these basic steps when playing fairway bunker shots.

- **Assessment** Always check that you have enough loft on your club to clear the bunker lip. It is more important to get out, than trying to commit to a shot that may get you all the way to your target.
- **Firm base, solid set-up** Place the ball near the centre of your stance, to give you a good clean strike of the ball. When setting-up always bury your feet into the ground until you find a good solid platform to swing a club from.
- **Good swing** Swing through the ball and consider an extra club when trying to hit a certain distance.

Gwladys Nocera of France plays from a fairway bunker on the 6th hole in Sun City.

The Old Course

The Old Course at St Andrews is the oldest golf course in the world and is considered the home of golf. St Andrews is steeped in history and has played a fundamental role in the evolution of the game of golf. The first record of golfing activities on this "common land" is in 1552, with the first game following some 22 years later in 1574. The Old Course is where the spirit and traditions of this noble game have been safeguarded for over five centuries.

▶ **fact**file

- CREATED **Over 500 years ago**
- LOCATION **St Andrews, Scotland**
- DISTANCE **6,721 yards**
- PAR **72**

The Old Course is a site of global importance and its traditions and status as one of the finest courses in the world are safeguarded by the Trustees. The Royal and Ancient Golf Club of St Andrews hold playing privileges on the course, as do the general public.

History

The course was originally host to only a handful of holes, with the game being played over the same set of fairways over and again. The popularity of the game increased as did the size of the course and the number of holes. By the 18th century, the course had increased in size to 22 holes, 11 out and 11 back. In 1764, some of the shorter holes were combined to relieve congestion, setting the standard for the 18-hole courses of today.

Layout and tradition

Only the 1st, 9th, 17th and 18th holes have their own greens, with all remaining holes enjoying two holes per double green, which can stretch up to 100 feet across. The course can be played either clockwise or anti-clockwise, although such play is carefully scheduled by the Trustees of the course. Anti-clockwise has become the accepted direction, though some of the bunkers have obviously been sited to catch players from the other direction.

The course is known for its particular physical features including 112 bunkers, some of which are especially famous, for example "Hell" on the long 14th, "Hill" and "Strath" on the short 11th and the "Road Bunker" at what is probably the most famous golf hole in the world, the 17th or "Road Hole" (so called because a road—which is in play—runs hard against the back edge of the green).

It is commonly known as the "Home of Golf," where golf was first played a mere 600 years ago, and yet it remains a real test of golf for today's elite, with its reputation and status feared and yet loved by so many.

Designed by nature

No single architect is credited with the design of St Andrews Links, instead it is the contribution of a variety of architects over the last six centuries that have made St Andrews Links the celebrated golf course it is today. The first course at St Andrews, The Old Course, is the oldest golf course in the world. It is Mother Nature who shaped the original course and gave it it's renowned physical features. In recent times Daw Anderson (1850s), Old Tom Morris (1860s–1900) and Dr Alister Mackenzie (1930s) have all played a role in the development of this course, to create what remains a true test of championship golf.

What you need...

The deep pot bunkers of St Andrews are the stuff of legend. But many great players, with good course management, avoid them. What players can never avoid—indeed don't want to—are the large, sometimes double, greens. (A "double" green serves two holes.) Their sheer size means that you could land your ball on the green yet still be 100 feet from the pin.

To play a very long putt you should follow your normal routine. Walk the green to assess how the ball will roll out, line it up as through you are going to hole it (imagine it's only 6 feet away!) and maintain a normal putting stroke except with a longer stroke. What will change, however, is the inclusion of wrists. By relaxing the wrists in the backswing you can allow a small amount of "cocking." In the downswing flick them forward;

this will allow the putter head to kick into the ball. This relaxed kick will propel the ball forward, giving it added distance, but will not change the natural stroke allowing you to maintain your rhythm and your aim.

The slight cocking and releasing of the wrists, unlike your normal putt, will give you extra distance over the green.

Winged Foot

Only 40 minutes from New York City's Grand Central Station, the town of Mamaroneck is the home to Winged Foot West, a grand and majestic course that has been at the centre of golf's traditions.

factfile

- CREATED **1923**
- LOCATION **New York, USA**
- DISTANCE **6,956 yards**
- PAR **72**

The Winged Foot courses were designed by A.W. Tillinghast in 1920 at the bequest of a group of men who were brought together by their shared association with the New York Athletic Club (NYAC). The club takes its name from the emblem of the NYAC and was opened three years later in 1923.

The "Championship" course

Winged Foot West was commissioned to be a "man-sized course" and one to rival the neighboring courses of Shinnecock Hills and The National, Long Island. This ideal has been realized—the course has six major championships, the most recent being the 2006 US Open.

Building the course

Building Winged Foot West was no mean feat. It took 220 workmen with horses and tractors to sculpt the magnificent 36 holes you see today. The courses' creators were dedicated to their vision of creating a prestigious course. The club house rises out from the tree line as a blend of earth and stone—a tip of the hat to the spectacular history of the land.

During the construction of the course, Mohegan Indians' stone arrowheads and other artefacts had been unearthed, together with items associated with the Revolutionary war, which would also have touched this area in the late 1700s.

Unlike on the East course, which is tighter and shorter, water does not come into play on the West. Yet with its intensely green and manicured grass, narrow fairways, deep rough, deep-set bunkers and doglegged holes, Winged Foot West demands accuracy of shots both from the tee and from fairway to green. Greenside bunkers lie in wait for the unwary, and the greens are highly contoured. Tillinghast's best example of this is found at the famous 10th hole, which he is said to have considered being his finest ever constructed. The rough is not a place to be, as the tree line pinches into the fairway.

Albert Warren Tillinghast

Albert Warren Tillinghast was born on 19th May 1874 and developed into one of the most prolific architects in golfing history. "Tillie" to those who knew him, was a crucial figure in the "Golden Age of Architecture" between the world wars. Tillinghast would have been the "catch of the day" for the Winged Foot gentlemen.

He designed a staggering 265 courses in his career—a number of those having hosted professional golf major championships, including Ceder Crest Park, Bethpage State Park, Ridgewood Country Club, and Baltusrol Golf Club.

What you need...

When playing West Winged Foot course you need to keep the ball straight and down the middle to avoid the heavy tree outline that shapes each golf hole. This will often leave you playing straight into the greens which some have a front side bunker for protection. When faced with a shot into a green guarded by a front side bunker it is easy to be deceived by how much space there is between the bunker and the green. Trust your yardages and ensure you have enough club to reach the green and that even with a bad shot you can clear that bunker.

As an aid it is sometimes nice to stick labels to the shaft of your clubs with the yardages written on them which show your average distance of that particular club. This will give you the confidence and reassurance to play your next shot with very little doubt as to whether the club will hit the ball far enough. Such an aid should also stop you trying to play the same shot as the person next to you who

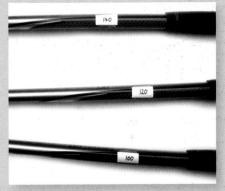

Of course you can remember your distances but in an anxious moment simple things such as labeling means that you have one less thing to think about—and this will help to boost your confidence.

always seems to take two clubs less. Do not fall into this trap; play within yourself and know the facts; this club will go this distance and this is the distance I have left into the green.

Know the rules... better

All golfers know some of the rules of golf; but very few know them all. One way to improve your scoring is to have a thorough understanding of certain key rules so that you can use them to your advantage. This is not cheating—not even gamesmanship—just having a sound knowledge for when you might need it.

On the tee

The rules are numerous and their interpretation can be tough.
They also change from time to time. The next few pages look just at
some parts of the rules that you may not know and which could cost
you—or save you—shots. The first and most important point to make
is that you must possess a copy of the full rules, produced jointly by
the R&A and the United States Golf Association. What follows is just a
selection of the most important things to observe.

Equipment

Players may carry 14 clubs, not necessarily
different; multiple wedges are allowed. The
penalties are significant:

- **stroke play**: two penalty shots per hole
  where the violation occurs up to a maximum
  of four shots
- **match play**: loss of hole on which the
  violation occurs up to a maximum of
  two holes
- **stableford**: deduct two points from the
  final score for each hole up to a maximum
  of four points.

  Also check your clubs and golf balls which
  must be "genuine." You are not allowed to
  play a practice or "cross out" ball. Starting
  play with any damaged club that does not
  conform, i.e. one with a dent in the shaft or
  a loose club head, is forbidden.

Cross out balls—for practice only.

Local rules

The rules of the Royal and Ancient Golf Club
(R&A) apply throughout the world of golf.
Individual courses, however, are entitled to add
"local rules." These primarily relate to special
local conditions, playing off paths, what is "out
of bounds," where you can drop etc. You
should check these before you start.

LOCAL RULES
Full details of Rules 4, 5 and 6 below are on the Local Rules
notice-boards outside the Professional's Shop and the
Clubhouse entrance to the men's locker room.
1. **OUT OF BOUNDS (Rule 27-1)**
   Beyond any boundary fence or hedge surrounding the
   course and beyond the white posts to the left of hole 1.
   Note: The road to the left of hole 1 is deemed to extend to
   the white posts.
2. **STONES IN BUNKERS (Rule 24-1)** are movable
   obstructions.
3. **TREES (Rule 24-2)** which are staked or protected with
   wrapping to be treated as immovable obstructions. Relief
   MUST be taken.
4. **GROUND UNDER REPAIR (Rule 25-1)**
   a) Relief MUST be taken from any area roped off or surrounded
   by a white line including temporary greens when preferred

5. **AERATION** Appendix 1. In brief: Re or slit. Throu to where it point that a
6. **IMMOVA SPRINKLE LENGTHS** Appendix Relief ava club-lengt line of pl interventi green.
   PENALT Match P1 Stroke P1

*Check the local rules, normally printed on the back of
your score card.*

Practice rules

Ever fancied a few holes before your
competition round? Beware.

- You may practise on the competition course
  before match play but *not* stroke play.
- You cannot practise prior to stroke play
  within the "boundary of the course," that is,
  anywhere the ball could legally end up.

- You cannot practise on the competition course between rounds in a two-round competition.

And did you know that during a round.
- You must not swing at anything resembling a ball!
- You can't chip onto the greens of holes just completed, the next tee, or to other players.
- You can't hit range balls back to tidy up a fairway.

Knocking your ball off the tee peg

Embarrassing yes, but not against the rules! A ball blown off the tee peg or accidentally knocked off during set-up, can be replaced without penalty. A shot is recorded If you have started your downswing and cannot stop, either just catching the ball or missing it.

Golfing aids

New technology is proving problematic. Golf teaching aids are excellent for improving your game in practice—but not in competition. Forbidden aids include:
- range finders
- devices for checking alignment at address (you can lie a club down)
- "swing straps" encouraging technically correct swings; if in doubt check with the club pro.

Tee markers

Golf courses mark tee boxes by coloured logs or "balls." Before a competition, check which colour tees you are using. A mistake can result in disqualification; you have effectively played the wrong course!

The teeing ground is a rectangle extending two club lengths backward from between the markers. The ball must be in this area, the player may stand outside.

Shots taken from outside the teeing ground do not count. Failure to return to the teeing ground before starting the next hole or departure from the 18th green, without rectifying the fault, results in disqualification.

You can stand anywhere but the ball must be in the marked area.

Conduct on the course
Shouting "Fore" Golf balls hurt! Protect other players. Don't be shy. It's far better to disturb the peace than risk injury.

Space on the tee It's courteous and safe to stand well away from your playing partners on the tee. Also do keep quiet; it's tempting to choose a club, take your glove off, comment on the course. But don't.

Lost and unplayable!

In competitions, all players have a duty to "protect the field," ensuring that everybody plays fairly and by the rules. To play your part, you need to give rules guidance with confidence, mainly to the person whose card you mark but also to anyone you come across on the course. Numerous situations arise in golf where the ball is unplayable. Below is a summary of the main ones, with guidance as to how to solve the problem while staying within the rules.

Searching for the ball

If your ball is lost you are allowed five minutes searching time. If found, play on. In match or stroke play if the ball is lost, return to the spot you played it from and play another. If this is on the tee, tee up in the normal way; if anywhere else, drop the ball and in all cases add one penalty shot plus the shot you would have been playing... hence, shot three if playing off the tee.

A time-saver is the "provisional" ball. Always declare the ball "provisional" before searching for the original. If found, the original must be played and the provisional ball abandoned. You can play on with the provisional without looking for your original ball but your opponent may choose to look and has five minutes in which to find it.

Hazards

You need to know the various definitions.

- **Ground under repair** This is marked by a GUR sign or lettering. You can drop at the nearest point of relief with no penalty.
- **Casual water** This comprises clearly visible water where the ball lies or where your stance would be. This means relief without penalty. Establish the nearest point that avoids the conditions and drop within one club length of that point. If in a bunker, take the nearest point that avoids the conditions or, if you prefer, drop the ball out of the bunker and incur a one shot penalty.
- **Water hazard (Yellow stakes)** If the ball is still playable (dry ditch), take no penalty but do not ground your club in the hazard. If unplayable, drop the ball anywhere behind the hazard, keeping the point where the ball last crossed the hazard between you and the hole. Penalty: one shot.
- **Water hazard (red stakes)** This is a lateral water hazard, running in the direction of play. Players may play the ball without grounding the club in the hazard. Otherwise, agree the line of entry with your marker and drop within two club lengths of the hazard. Penalty: one shot. An alternative is to drop on the other side of the hazard. In either case, the drop must be no nearer the hole.
- **Groundstaff cuttings and clippings** Drop within one club length of nearest point of relief from interference, no penalty.

All of the above apply in a bunker though you may not drop outside the bunker. In all cases, a one-shot penalty applies.

Finally, the ball may also be unplayable—being cracked, cut, or out of shape. It can be replaced, without penalty, but this should be cleared with your marker.

Conduct on the course

Avoid slow play Stay up with the group ahead and invite groups through if you have to spend more than a few moments looking for your ball.

Playing the unplayable ball

You are the sole judge of an unplayable ball and nobody can disagree! Three options follow:

1 Play a ball from the spot where the unplayable ball was last played.

2 Drop a ball within two club lengths of the unplayable ball, no nearer the hole.

3 Drop a ball behind the point where the ball lies, keeping that point directly between the hole and the spot on which the ball is dropped.

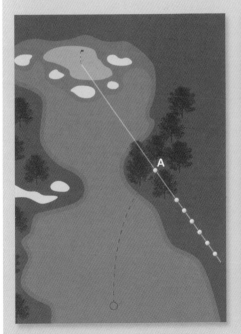

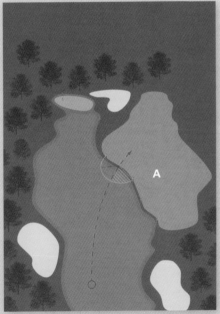

You find your ball in the trees (A) and decide it's unplayable. If dropping the ball two club lengths from its position you have the option of taking it back anywhere on the line behind the ball and in line with the flag.

The ball has entered the lateral water hazard (A). Agreement has to be reached on where the ball entered. The drop is made two club lengths from this point but no nearer the hole.

Can't play the ball?

Although a lost ball, problems in hazards, and the unplayable ball will account for most of the "ball" problems on the course, there are some other situations where a clear knowledge of the rules is also helpful.

Loose impediments and obstructions

- **Loose impediments** are natural things e.g. leaves, pine cones.
- **Obstructions** (movable and immovable) are man-made and must be on the course.

You may move loose impediments except when your ball is in a hazard but beware: If the ball moves as a result there is a one-shot penalty.

You may remove movable obstructions e.g. a 150-yard marker, and if the ball moves as a result there is no penalty and the ball must be replaced. If you cannot move the obstruction, then you may move the ball (free drop), but only if the obstruction is interfering with your stance, the ball, or the area of your intended swing. If an immovable object is in the line of your shot—that's tough.

Staked trees

Young trees are vulnerable and need protection from club and ball. If staked, players may take relief without penalty, dropping the ball within one club length from the nearest point of relief, that is, the nearest point at which the tree will not be hit by a normal swing. As always when dropping, the ball must come to rest no nearer the hole.

1 This obstruction (a wall) is man-made but is clearly immovable. If it impedes your stroke that is unfortunate; there is no relief. The same applies if it is in your line of shot. 2 A movable obstruction (the marker), is simply that and may be shifted. It's important you read local rules about what is "movable" and "immovable."

Be your own referee

When you note a penalty on yourself always declare it to the others in your group. Do not hide from it, as it will only play on your mind and may cause you bad shots. Try to move on from this moment and do not allow your group to mention it more than is required—you need to have a clear head for your next shot.

Animal scraping

Wildlife inhabiting a golf course not only adds to the attraction but also presents interesting rule situations. Holes or runways made by burrowing animals or birds which interfere with your shot mean relief without penalty, one club length from the nearest point of relief, no nearer the hole.

Ball plugged

Under "winter rules," which may apply at different times for different courses, you may be allowed to clean and place a ball which is "plugged" on the fairway, within six inches but no nearer the hole. A ball falling into long grass may well be plugged but will not provide relief.

Dropping the ball

Many of the situations described in the last few pages require you to drop the ball to restart the round. There are clear rules as to how this should be done in order to ensure that you do not seek to gain any advantage from the situation.

The following procedure should be followed.

- Player stands upright.
- Ball held at shoulder level and arms length.
- Ball must be redropped with no penalty if it touches the player, other players, or equipment.
- Do not drop the ball nearer the hole.
- Drop the ball vertically and without spin.
- Drops without penalty (free drop) should be within one club length.
- Drops with one-shot penalty (e.g. after entering a hazard) should be within two club lengths.
- If the ball comes to rest outside the designated area it should be redropped. If it

happens for a second time, the ball should be placed as near to the spot where it hit the course on the second attempt.

Scorecard faults

You have responsibilities in terms of recording scores and presenting an accurate scorecard. You should:

- accurately record the scores of your opponent, having switched cards
- ensure that the correct handicap is recorded on the card before handing in
- sign your own card as a player and your opponent's as marker
- hand your scorecard in without delay.

Disqualification will result from recording a lower score than taken for any hole or from a player not signing the card. If the score signed for is higher, it stands. Professionals make these mistakes from time to time, so take care!

Professionals practice dropping! Remember to mark the ground where you are dropping to ensure the ball comes to rest within the appropriate distance and no nearer the hole.

Don't get penalized

Putting together a decent score is tough enough; throwing away shots through penalties makes it hard to compete, and it hits morale. Your playing partner may help you with rules advice but you must not rely on this. You should be sure of the rules yourself.

Giving and taking advice

"Great shot—what did you use there?," "You need to keep it down the left here," and "There's a lot of wind up there today"… innocent remarks maybe but they constitute seeking advice, giving advice, or influencing others are all against the rules. Coaching an opponent during a competition round is also not allowed.

Can you discuss anything with the opposition? Yes. "Is the pin at the front of the green or the back?" is an allowable question. This is public knowledge and the player is entitled to it. Similarly, information on rules is not advice. Outline the options for an unplayable ball but do not advise on which option is best.

So where do you get help? Your partner, caddie or your partner's caddie are all legal allies. Observation is the key word. If your caddie spots a club missing from the opponent's bag, he can tell you; it may influence club selection but he can't rummage through the bag to find out! Caddies and partners can go ahead and indicate the line on a blind shot and even place a marker provided it is removed before the shot is played. The flagstick can be held up at any time to indicate the hole position.

Mistakes in this area can be costly: loss of hole in match play, two-shot penalty in stroke play.

Bunkers

The greatest players in the world are trapped by well-placed bunkers; the handicap golfer certainly will be. The objective is to get out first time without further penalty and continue your round. There are clear rules.

- The sand should not be touched before playing the ball. This includes raking the sand for another player before playing your ball and also includes your own backswing.
- The club may not be grounded in the sand when addressing the ball.

Errors here will result in a two-shot penalty in stroke play and loss of hole in match play.

Identifying your ball and playing the wrong ball

A problem area for amateur players. The rules are clear however. Players may lift, without penalty, a ball they believe to be their own in order to identify it. They should tell their marker, opposition, or fellow competitors that they intend to do this and allow them to

Conduct on the course

Ready to go! Be ready to play when it's your turn; a good flow to the game helps everybody and will stop you over-analysing each shot.

observe it. The ball can be cleaned but only to help identification including the removal of sand from the ball in a bunker.

Penalties for playing the wrong ball will hurt your chances: loss of hole in match play, two-shot penalty in stroke play. A recent rule change says you should identify your ball in a hazard too— previously this was not the case.

A solution to much of the above is mark your ball clearly before play and tell your opponents what that marking is.

Even if your ball has significant markings such as logos and advertising it's still worth putting your own identifying marks on it.

Eric Axley walks to identify his ball after a fan finally found it among deep rough in the woods on the 4th hole during the third round of the John Deere Classic at TPC at Deere Run in Silvis, Illinois

Take extra care

As well as advice violations, indiscretions in bunkers and ball identification, there are other key areas to be aware of during play.

Ball at rest moved

Be careful when you are around your ball; you could incur penalties. If you should accidentally move your ball, lift it when not permitted, or it moves after you address it, you should add one penalty stroke, replace your ball, and play on.

You must make sure you replace the ball. If you don't you lose the hole in match play or a total of two shots in stroke play. If someone else moves your ball or their ball moves yours, replace it without penalty.

Referee (John Paramor) gives Michael Campbell of New Zealand a ruling during the WGC American Express Championship. Whatever the situation the key advice is never to touch your ball unless you are certain of the rules and you have the agreement of other plays and officials.

Conduct on the course

Keep quiet when partners are playing. Good concentration is essential for good golf.

Ball in motion deflected or stopped

There are three main situations here, all of which highlight the need to pay attention to where you stand with fellow competitors, opponents, partners, and caddies.

- You, your partner, or caddie must not stop or deflect a ball you have played.
- If your ball hits your opponent or their caddie (or vice versa) that's unfortunate but no penalty is incurred.
- If a ball hit by you is deflected or stopped by another ball then there is no penalty except in stroke play when your ball and another were both on the green; this results in a two-shot penalty.

The best advice therefore is to stand to the side and slightly behind playing partners. This reduces the risk of getting hit. Also request that other players mark their ball when you are putting.

Improving your lie

"Play the ball as it lies" is a principle understood by most golfers. Handicap golfers are less circumspect when it comes to improving their lie. You should not improve your stance area, your intended swing area, or your line of play by bending or breaking anything fixed or growing. This includes pressing anything down when taking your stance. Club players frequently do this, not necessarily seeking to gain advantage but out of lack of rules knowledge. It could cost you dear; the penalty is loss of hole in match play or two shots in stroke play.

Once you've addressed it, the slightest movement of the ball is deemed to be a stroke and counts as one shot.

Know where you are

Making the wrong decision can cost you dearly in situations like these.

Fringe   Green

G.U.R   Course

O.O.B   Course

O.O.B   Course

A A part of the ball is touching the green so you are on the green and may lift your ball.

B Part of the ball is touching the line so you are in the Ground Under Repair and can drop your ball.

C The inside line of Out Of Bounds is in the course—but no part of the ball is touching this so you are out of bounds.

D part of your ball is over the inside line of Out Of Bounds so you are in luck!

On the green

Etiquette, the unwritten code of conduct, is possibly more important on the greens than anywhere else. There are fewer two-shot penalties to be avoided but your reputation as a playing companion is at stake.

The etiquette

It's best to remember how important good behaviour is.

- Always leave your trolley, buggy, or bag well clear of the putting surface.
- Avoid any scuffing of the green with spikes.

There's always a lot happening on and around the green. Take care and be aware of both your movement and your equipment. This applies also when you are walking past a green that others are playing. This is the scene at The Presidents Cup at The Royal Montreal Golf Club in Quebec, Canada.

- Stand well away from, and to the side of, players putting so as to avoid both their line of sight and any accusations about gaining information for your putt.
- Never walk on the line of another player's putt. Mark your ball if in doubt.
- When attending the flag, ensure it comes out easily to avoid penalty situations.
- Remain still and quiet while people are putting.

... and the rules

It is worth checking your knowledge of putting green rules.

- You can mark, lift, and clean your ball at any time without penalty.
- The marker should be flat; use of tee pegs or pitch mark repairers is not illegal but not recommended.
- Having marked your ball, you can be asked to move the marker to avoid interfering with the line of another player's putt. The marker must be replaced in the original spot to avoid a two-shot penalty.
- If you hit the flag staff you will be penalised, whether the flag is in the hole or lying on the green: two shots in stroke play, loss of hole in match play.
- In match play, if you hit your opponent's ball with your putt, you lose the hole. In stroke play you are penalized two shots. Your shot is played as it lies, the other ball replaced.

- You can repair ball mark damage, but not spike marks.
- If your ball is on the lip, you are allowed "a reasonable amount of time to reach the ball" followed by a further ten seconds. If the ball has not dropped the ball must be played. Failure to do this results in a one-shot penalty.
- If your ball is standing in casual water on the green, you can move it clear of the water without penalty. The same applies if there is water between your ball and the flag. In both cases the ball must be placed no nearer the hole.

Always have a set of rules in your bag. Your club should have copies and now you can also download them for free from the Internet.

Be particularly careful

- Don't leave your bag where it might be deemed an aid to working out the line of a putt.
- If you are indicating the line of a putt to your partner don't tap the ground with your putter; you can't touch the line of the putt.
- If it's windy be very careful about grounding your club before your shot. Once you've done this, and the ball moves, that's a shot. If in doubt, do not address the ball.
- Pick loose impediments off the green in your line; don't brush them away or pat down the ground (unless repairing a ball mark).

Conduct on the course

Pitch marks Repair your own and one other every time you visit a green.

Reference

Glossary

A

Address—position when standing over the ball, with the club grounded and the stance completed

Aim point—a straight line from your ball to the target point

Aiming away—a straight shot to go past a hazard

Aiming off—avoiding a hazard by shaping your shot away from it

Aiming over—flying the ball over the hazard

Albatross—three under par on a single hole

Arc of the putt—the club angle between fully-back and follow-through, ideally one third back and two thirds through

Attack point—the best position from which to reach your target

Avenue—a practice-ground drill where all the clubs are used to test distance and accuracy by hitting balls down an imaginary "avenue"

B

Backspin—spinning the ball backwards, created by the angle of attack and the club speed, to stop the ball dead

Backwards shot—playing one-handed, for short distance shots

Ball shaping—produces either a fade or a draw

Ball spin—created by the clubface and allows the ball to hook, fade, slice or draw

Belly putter—allows you to anchor the putter in your abdomen

Birdie—one under par on a single hole

Bogey—one over par on a single hole

Borrows—slopes or other irregularities in the green, similar to "breaks"

Bounce/Bounce angle—the angle between the club face at address and that part of the club actually touching the ground—determines how much contact the club face makes with the ground

Break—where the ball begins to move off-line when putting over the contours of the green

Broom-handle putter—long-handled putter that creates a complete pendulum when in an upright stance

Bump and run—usually played with a 7, 8 or 9 iron and similar to the chip shot but with less loft and more "run"

C

CARVE—an acronym to establish optimum control of your game: Controlled, Adaptable, Realistic, Visionary, Efficient

Casting the club—players who self-correct their swing plane during the stroke

Cavity back—a scooped-out back of the club distributes the weight around the perimeter

Centre shaft (putter)—the shaft is exactly in the centre of the putter head, to maintain an even balance between toe and heel

Chip shot—used from off the green to drop the ball short of the target and to let it roll the rest of the way

Clicker—paces counter

Closed clubface—the toe of the club is turned inward—tends to produce a hook or pull

Closed stance—clubface square to target, feet angled inside parallel

Connected swing—good body rotation combined with effective transfer of weight

Course review—an analysis of each hole played and the lessons that can be learnt from that analysis

Cut shot—produces a controlled fade

D

Distance awareness—knowing exactly where you are on the hole

Distance game—all strokes from the tee to the approach shot

Divot—that part of the turf dislodged when hitting a pitch shot in the correct "ball-to-turf" order to create backspin

Double bogey—two over par on a single hole

Double eagle—an Albatross

Downhill lie—with the ball on a downslope it is best to club-down to increase the distance the ball will fly

Draw—a shot that starts to the right but then deviates to the left (right-handed player)

E

Eagle—two under par on a single hole

F

Fade—a shot that starts to the left but then deviates to the right (right-handed player)

Fat/heavy—hitting the turf first (not the ball), usually during a pitch, chip, or lob shot

Flyer, get a—the wrong clubface-to-ball contact when playing out of the rough

Fore!—a "watch out" shout to warn other players that they may be hit by your ball

G

Goal focus—the ability to find a reason for what you do, and why you do it

Grand Slam—winning the four Majors: The US Open, The British Open, The Masters and The US PGA in the same year

H

Handicap—a calculated over-par expectation for your round

Handrailing—using a course feature that lines a hole as a guide for your shot

Heavy/fat—hitting the turf first (not the ball), usually during a pitch, chip, or lob shot

Hogan-Slam—winning The US Open, The British Open and The Masters in the same year

Hook—the ball flight begins right but then veers dramatically to the left (right-handed player), missing the target by a long way—the opposite of the slice

Hybrid club—an iron-style club face with a wood-style bulb behind

Hydration—the source of fluid that maintains body temperature

I

Idolization—hero worship

Immediate focus—good technique and decision-making, giving you the ability to enter your exclusive "zone of excellence"

Impact—the point where you actually strike the ball

In the zone—those moments producing excellence where anything is possible

Indirect Putting—a drill to allow you to work on your putting skill by deliberately missing the hole but keeping to within two feet of it

K

Kick point—where the shaft flexes the most (varies with each club)

L

Launch angle—the angle at which the ball leaves the club head

Lie angle—the angle between the centre of the shaft and the sole of the club

Loading—the transfer of weight to the right side (right-handed player) by rotating the hips and shoulders

Lob shot—is an advance pitch shot where the ball lands almost vertically and stops dead

Local rules—additions to R&A rules that apply only to one specific course

Loft—the angle on the clubface that causes the ball to rise

Low ball—move the ball slightly back in the stance to maintain distance in a strong wind

M

Majors—The US Open, The British Open, The Masters and The US PGA Championships

Match Play—playing against an opponent in a hole-by-hole format

N

Nutrition—the energy taken from food and nourishment

O

Offset—the shaft is positioned in front of the club head

Offset toe-and-heal (putter)—the putter has an angled S-shape neck between the shaft and the head

One- (to -four) piece ball—the number of layers (more layers = better quality)

Open clubface—the toe of the club is turned rearward—tends to produce a push or slice

Open stance—clubface square to target, feet angled outside parallel

Orienteering—thinking about all aspects of the hole, using course maps and other course aids

Overloading—overloaded muscle will be strengthened only when forced to operate beyond natural tolerances

P

Pace of the green—the speed at which putts will travel

Pacing out—working out distances by the number of strides taken

Par—the number of strokes a scratch player should take at any hole

Par-18 practice—with nine balls placed around a green, hole out in two shots with each ball

Par-27 practice—over nine holes, drop a ball 70–180 yards from the pin and hole out in no more than three shots at each hole

Parallel alignment—having the feet, hips and shoulders all square to the club face position

Pitch shot—used from off the green, with a high-loft iron, to create backspin and stop the ball dead

Play line—a personal drill used to focus before addressing the ball; an imaginary "point of no return"

Play-Off—extra holes played where two or more players have tied for the lead after the final round

Plugged ball—ball hardly visible in a hazard

Plus-one practice—you are allowed one extra stroke to hit the green before holing out in regulation

Preparation zone—getting mentally and physically ready for the golf shot by blocking out all other thoughts

Pull—a ball hit in a straight line well to the left of the target line (right-handed player)—the opposite of a push

Pull back—a putting-practice drill which avoids repeating the same putt

Pure-ing—a technique used to determine the correct shaft alignment in relation to the head

Push—a ball hit in a straight line well to the right of the target line (right-handed player)—the opposite of a pull

Putter head face inserts—attachments to the putter face to create a different ball reaction

R

Reactive targeting—assessing the options and choosing the best landing area for a golf shot

Release and roll—a chip shot without backspin

Repeatability—the ability to reproduce any given shot over and over again

Rescue club—another name for a hybrid club

Reverse shot—using the clubface, turn the toe of the club towards you and strike the ball

S

Set-up—physical and mental awareness when addressing the ball in a manner which allows you to aim straight at your target

Shaft and butt weighting (putter)—the ability to adjust the swing weight and the overall dead weight of the putter

Shaping the shot—closing or opening the club face to produce either a draw or fade

Short game—putting, plus any approach shots from within 100–150 yards of the green

Slice—the ball flight begins left but then veers dramatically to the right (right-handed player) missing the target by a long way—the opposite of a hook

Specificity—the ability to improve a range of movement within a particular body area

Stance—the setting of the feet prior to the stroke

Standard putter—allows you to lean over the ball and to have a palm-to-palm grip

Stroke play—counting the number of shots taken in a round to determine the winner

Strong grip—the V between the thumb and forefinger is pointing to the right shoulder (right-handed player)

Sweet spot—that part of any club head where maximum power is generated

Swing plane—the path that the club takes to the top of the backswing and then back to and through impact

T

Target line—a straight line to the target

Target point—where you want the ball to land (rarely the flag!)

Toe hung—the club has the heaviest part of its mass in the toe

Toe-and-heel weighting (putter)—the weight is concentrated in both ends of the putter

Trigger mechanism—a mannerism or routine that is carried out before every shot

Tunnel—a chip- (or pitch-) and-run practice drill using golf clubs on the ground to form a "tunnel"

Twitch, fast—muscle fibres developed with exercises for muscular strength

Twitch, slow—muscle fibres that use oxygen to deliver "fuel" for long-lasting energy

U

Up and down—taking only two shots to hole-out from close to, but not on, the green

Uphill lie—with the ball on an upslope it is best to take an extra club as the ball will lose distance with higher elevation

V

Visualization—a mental picture of the execution of the entire stroke, beginning with address and ending with the ball landing in the target area and rolling to a stop

W

Weak grip—the V between the thumb and forefinger is pointing to the chin, rather than to the right shoulder (right-handed player)

Weight transfer—the movement of weight from loading, at takeaway, through impact to follow-through

Wrong-handed shot—playing the opposite way to normal using the back of the club

Y

Yips—nervousness, especially when putting

Z

Zone, in the—that period of time when every shot is perfectly thought through and executed

Index

A

Address 56, 71, 82, 84, 86, 90, 103, 201, 209
Age, shoot below 15
Aiming off 160–175
Anderson, Daw 195
Animal hazards 205
Arc of the putt 55–56
Attack/Attack point 156, 166–167, 175
Augusta National 12, 75, 178–179, 191
Avenue practice 155
Axley, Eric 207

B

Backspin 66–69, 106
Backswing 67
Backwards shot 101
Bags 130–131
Ball motion 58–59
Ball shaping 154
Ball spin 135
Balls 130, 140–141, 200–211
Belly putter 53, 140
Bich, Baron Marcel 182
Borrows 54
Bounce/Bounce angle 134–135
Braid, James 180–181
British Amateur Championship 12
British Ladies' Open Championship 18, 28
British Open Championship 12, 14, 16, 20, 22–26, 30
British Seniors' Open Championship 22
Broom-handle putter 53, 140

Bump and run 65, 70–71, 134, 152
Bunkers/Bunker shots 23, 106–107

C

Campbell, Michael 208
Carbohydrates 116–118, 191
CARVE 44–47
Casual water 202, 211
Cavity back 135
Celebration 60, 75
Centre shaft 139
Chip shot 64–65, 68–69, 134, 136–137, 152
Clickers 143
Clothing 144–145
Club choice 99
Club head 135
Club head speed 13, 17, 31, 69, 73, 78, 90–91, 107, 135, 187
Clubs—see Equipment
Coaches/Coaching 26–27, 42–43, 82, 84, 86, 149
Commitment line 78–79, 149
Competitions 36–37
Confidence 31
Connected swing 91
Continuous swing 91
Course management 160–175
    Ability level 164
    Aiming off 170–171
    Attack point 156, 166–167, 175
    Club distance 173
    Course map 163
    Course review 174–175

Distance awareness 172–173
    Handrailing 168–169
    Hazards and features 164
    Orienteering 162, 165
    Outcomes 165
    Pacing 172–173
    Pre-conceptions 162
    Reactive targeting 164–166, 175
    Scorecard and stats 175
    Strategy 162–163
    The next shot 165
    Yards or metres 173
Courses (Great ones) 176–19
    Augusta National 178–179
    Gleneagles 180–181
    Les Bordes 182–183
    Muirfield Village 184–185
    Pebble Beach 186–187
    Pine Valley 188–189
    Royal Melbourne 190–191
    Sun City 192–193
    The Old Course (St. Andrews) 194–195
    Winged Foot 196–197
Crump, George 188–189
Cut shot 100
Cuttings/Clippings 202–203

D

Diet 111, 117
Distance awareness 172–173
Divots 67
Downhill lie 102–103
Draw 89, 92–93
Drills—see Practice
Driver 128, 132–134

E

Egan, Henry 187

Els, Ernie 23, 79

Equipment 126–145, 200

Bags and trolleys 130–131

Bag contents 130

Ball spin 135

Balls 130, 140–141, 200–211

Bounce/Bounce angle 135–137

Buying new clubs 36–37, 128–129

Caps, hats and visors 145

Cavity back 135

Clothing 104, 130, 144–145

Club head 135

Club head cleaner 142

Equipment upgrades 36, 128

Gloves 104, 130, 144

Irons 128, 134–135

Launch angle 135

Lie angle 135

Loft 134–135

Offset 135

Pure-ing 135

Putters (see separate entry)

Rule book 142

Scorecard and yardage book 142

Shaft flex 135

Shoes 144

Tees 130, 142

Towels 130, 142

Umbrellas 130

Wedges (see separate entry)

Woods (see separate entry)

Yardage clickers and rangefinders 143

Exercises 120–125

F

Fade 89, 92–93

Faldo, Nick 26–27

Fat 117

Feedback 39

Feel-good factor 39

Fisher, Ross 47

Fitness for golf 15, 19, 31, 108–125

Aerobic endurance 111–113

Basics 110–111

Fast twitch muscles 114

Golf-specific exercises 120–125

Hydration 113

Muscular fitness 111, 114–115, 118, 120–125

Nutrition (see separate entry)

Slow twitch muscles 114–115

Training programs (see separate entry)

Focus 13–14, 31, 34–35, 37, 40–41, 43–44, 47, 50–51, 61, 75, 78–79, 83, 91, 114, 148–151, 156, 158

Follow-through 13, 56, 87

Fore! 201

Furyk, Jim 32

G

Game plan 37, 40–41, 46

Garcia, Sergio 10

Gleneagles 24, 180–181

Goal focus 35–36

Goals 35, 42, 183

Grand Slam 12, 24

Great courses—see Courses

Great players 10–31

Grips 80–82, 90, 99, 133, Vardon 80

Ground under repair 202

H

Hall of Fame 22, 27

Handrailing 168–169

Harmon, Butch 43

Harrington, Padraig 137

Hazards 65, 69, 96, 98–101, 104–107, 164, 166, 170, 173

Hogan, Ben 15–17, 24

Hogan Slam 16

Hook shot 100

Hybrids 138, 133–134

Hydration 113

I

Idolization 36, 38–39

Immediate focus 35

Impact 13, 19, 56, 67, 79, 87–88, 90

Indirect putting 150

Irons 128, 134–135

J

Jones, Bobby 12–13, 18, 22, 178–179

K

Karlsson, Robert 50, 189

Kim, Anthony 60

L

Launch angle 135

Leadbetter, David 26–27
Les Bordes 182–183
Lewis, Stacy 170
Lie angle 135
Lies 102–103, 106–107, 148, 169, 209
Loading 86
Lob shot 65, 72–73, 106, 134, 136–137
Local rules 200
Loft 21, 67, 73, 92, 103, 136, 138, 193
Lord, Gareth 189
Lost and unplayable! 100–101, 202–203

M

MacKenzie, Dr. Alister 178, 190–191, 195
Maiden, Jimmy 12
Mannerisms 45, 94–95
Maslow's Hierarchy 183
Masters, The 12, 14–16, 20, 22–27, 30, 75, 178–170, 184
McCormack, Mark 21
Mediate, Rocco 55
Mental drills 148–149
Mickelson, Phil 43, 64
Mind game, The 23, 31–47, 148–149
   Attitude 40
   Competition 36–37
   Focus 34–35
   Goals 35
   Idolization 36, 38–39
   Lessons 42–43
   Managing your game 43–47
   Off-course practice 42–43

Pressure 37
Recognition 39
Your approach 40–41
Montgomerie, Colin 34
Morcom, Mick 190
Morris, Tom 195
Motivation 36
Movement dynamics 54, 56–58, 64–65
Muirfield Village 184–185
Murray, Henry 35
Muscles 111–112, 114–115, 118

N

Natural stroke 56, 58
Nelson, Byron 16
Neville, Jack 186–187
Nicklaus, Jack 11, 16, 24–26, 31, 38, 181, 184–185, 187
Nocera, Gwladys 193
Nutrition 116–118, 191
   Carbohydrates 116–117, 191
   Diet and nutrition 111, 117
   Fat 117
   Protein 117
   Timing of food 117

O

O'Hair, Sean 88
Ochoa, Lorena 19, 29
Offset 135
Offset toe and heel 139
Old Course, The (St. Andrews) 194–195
Orienteering 162, 165
Out of bounds 209
Out of trouble 96–107

Overloading 118

P

Pacing 172–173
Palmer, Arnold 20–21, 24, 27
Par 18 practice 153
Par 27 practice 156
Paramor, John 208
Pebble Beach 186–187
Penalties—see Rules
Perfect score/Perfect round 29, 78, 98
PGA Championship 14, 16, 22, 24, 30
PGA Seniors' Championship 14, 20, 22, 24
Pine Valley 188–189
Pinnick, Harvey 60
Pitch shot 65–67, 106, 134, 136–137
Play line 78–79, 149
Player, Gary 22–23, 35, 64, 192–193
Players (Greatest) 10–31
Plugged ball 205
Plus-one practice 157
Poulter, Ian 62, 93
Practice 40–43, 45, 47, 50, 73, 75, 78, 82, 87, 91, 102, 114, 146–159,
   Between matches 158–159
   Mental drills 148–149,
   On the course 156–157
   Planning 158–159
   Post-match 158–159
   Pre-match 158
   Putting 61, 150–151
   The short game 73, 75, 152–153

The swing 78, 154–155
Practice rules 200–201
Preparation zone 45
President's Cup 190, 210
Pressel, Morgan 143
Protein 117
Pull back 149
Pure-ing 135
Putter head/Putter loft 21, 54,
    58 (see also: Equipment)
Putters 51–53, 138–140
    Belly putter 53, 140
    Broom–handle putter 53, 140
    Centre shaft 139
    Grip shape 53, 138
    Grip size 138
    Length 139
    Lie angle 138
    Loft 21, 138
    Offset toe and heel 139
    Putter head 138
    Putter head face inserts 138
    Shaft and butt weighting 54,
        139
    Standard putter 53, 140
    Toe and heel weighting 139
    Toe hung 138
Putting 25, 48–61, 195 (see also:
    Practice; Equipment)
    Ball at rest 56, 58
    Ball motion 58–59
    Basics 50–51
    Celebration 60
    Feel and rhythm 61
    Focus 60–61
    Movement dynamics 54,
        56–58
    Natural stroke 56, 58
    Observation 60

Set up 60
Set-up 51–53, 56–57, 61
Stroke 50, 54–55, 57
Stroke 58–61
Sweet spot 54
The Grip 52–53
The perfect putt 60–61
Using technology 59

R
Range, on the 148–159
Reactive targeting 164–166, 175
Repeatability 13, 51, 57, 59, 61,
    64–65, 78, 89, 94
Reverse shot 101
Roberts, Clifford 178
Roberts, Loren 74
Rose, Justin 96
Rough—see Hazards
Routine 45, 94–95
Royal and Ancient Gold Club
    (R&A) 194, 200
Royal Melbourne 190–191
Rules 54, 142, 198–211
    Can't play the ball? 100–101,
        204–205
    Lost and unplayable!
        100–101, 202–203
    On the tee 200–201
    On the green 210–211
    Penalties 100–101, 106,
        206–209
    Rule book 142
Russell, Alex 190
Ryder Cup, The 26, 39, 180, 185

S
Sakurai, Yoshiaki 182
Sarazen, Gene 18
Scorecard 142, 205
Self-correction 13, 89
Set-up 51–53, 56–57, 61
Shaft and butt weighting 54,
    139
Shaft flex 132–133
Shaping a shot 92–93, 171
Shoes 144–145
Short game, The 23, 62–75,
    134, 152–153
    Backspin 67
    Bump and run 65, 70–71,
        134, 152
    Celebration 75
    Chip shot 64–65, 68–69,
        134, 136–137, 152
    Divots 67
    Execution 74–75
    Feel 75
    Focus 75
    Hitting with the toe 71
    Lob shot 65, 72–73, 106,
        134, 136–137
    Movement dynamics 64–65
    Observation 75
    Pitch or chip? 69
    Pitch shot 65–67, 106, 134,
        136–137
    Principles 65
    Putter or iron? 71
    Set-up 75
    Swing speed 73
    Use your imagination 64–65
    Wedges 73
    Wrist movement 69
Shot choice 99

Shoulder-hip ratio 17
Snead, Sam 14–15, 23, 27, 31
Sorenstam, Annika 28–29
Specificity 118–125
St. Andrews—The Old Course
    12, 25, 191, 194–195
Stance 84–85, 90
Standard putter 53, 140
Stenson, Henrik 164
Strategy 162–163
Strike 17, 25, 88–91, 99, 101,
    193
Stroke 58–61
Sun City 192–193
Suneson, Fanny 164
Sweet spot 54
Swing plane 13, 17, 78, 84,
    87–90
Swing ratio 17
Swing speed 73
Swing, The 15, 17, 27, 31, 41,
    73, 76–95, 102–104, 114,
    193
    Alignment 82–83
    Checking and correcting 89
    Club head speed 90
    Connected swing 91
    Continuous swing 13
    Feel, set–up and execution
        13, 94–95
    Impact 90–91
    Myth of 78–79
    Perfect parallel alignment 83
    Repeatability 78–79
    Routine 83
    Shaping the shot 92–93, 171
    Stance and posture 84–85,
        90

Swing plane 13, 17, 78, 84,
    87–90
The grip 80–82, 90
Visualization 85
Weak and strong (grips) 81
Weight transfer 86–87

T
Takeaway 13, 78, 86–87, 89
Target line 92
Targeting 164–166, 175
Tee markers 201
Tees 142
Tillinghast, Albert 196–197
Timing 13–14
Toe and heel weighting 139
Toe hung 138
Tomasulo, Peter 104
Towel 142
Training programs 118–125
    Adaptation 118
    Muscles 111–112, 114–115,
        118
    Overloading 118
    Recovery 118
    Reversibility 119
    Specificity 118
Traps 106–107
Trees, staked 204
Trigger mechanism 45, 94–95
Trolleys 130–131
Trouble, Getting out of
    96–107
    Attitude 105
    Backwards shot 101
    Balance 102
    Ball above feet 103

Ball below feet 103
Ball strike 99
Club choice 99
Cut shot 100
Downhill lie 102–103
Fairway bunker shots 107
Greenside bunker shots
    106–107
Hook shot 100
Planning the shot 105
Poor conditions 104–105
Rain 104
Reverse shot 101
Rough 98
Shot choice 99
Slopes 102–103
Steep angle 99
The grip 99
The low ball 105
Traps 106–107
Trees and obstacles 100–101
Uphill lie 102–103
Wind 104–105
Wrong-handed shot 101
Tunnel practice 152
Twitch, fast and slow 114–115

U
Umbrellas 130
Uphill lie—see Lies
US Amateur Championship 12,
    20, 24, 30, 185, 187
US Open Championship 12, 14,
    16, 20, 22, 24, 30, 50, 55,
    187, 189, 196
US PGA Championship 14, 16,
    22, 24, 30

US PGA Seniors' Open
  Championship 14, 20, 22, 24
US Women's Open
  Championship 18, 28, 170

V
Van de Velde, Jean 182
Vardon grip 80
Villegas, Camilo 76, 115
Visualization 25, 45, 85, 93, 148
von Hagge, Robert 182–183

W
Walker Cup 188
Water hazards 202
Wedges 66–73, 84, 106–107,
  134, 136–137, 173
  Angles 136

Bounce/Bounce angle
  136–137
Sand wedges 136–137
Sets 136
Weight transfer 13, 78, 84,
  86–87
Wethered, Joyce 18
Williams, Serena 94
Winged Foot 196–197
Woods 128, 132–134
  Driver head 132
  Fairway woods 128, 133
  Height and flex 133
  Shaft flex 132–133
  The driver 14, 128, 132
  The grip 133
  The hybrid 128, 133–134
Woods, Tiger 11, 16, 19, 25,
  30–31, 38, 64, 75, 90, 110,
  172

Woosnam, Ian 140
World Golf Hall of Fame 22, 27
World Matchplay Championship
  22
Wrong-handed shot 101

Y
Yardage 143, 189

Z
Zaharias, Babe 11, 18–19
Zone, in the 35

The following photographs are all courtesy of Getty Images:

p7 Stuart Franklin; p9 Lonny Kalfus; pp 10–11 Warren Little; p12 Kirby; p14 Getty Images; p16 Hulton Archive/Stringer; p 19 William Vanderson; p 20 Popperfoto/Contributor; p 22 Sam Greenwood; p 24 PGA Tour Photo Services/Contributor; p 26 Stuart Franklin; p 28 Paul Kane; p 30 Andrew Redington; pp 32–33 Marco Garcia; p 34 Andrew Redington; p 38 Hunter Martin; p 43 Richard Heathcote; p 47 Andrew Redington; pp 48–49 Robyn Beck; p 50 Doug Pensinger; p 55 Robyn Beck; p 60 Richard Heathcote; pp 62–63 Nick Laham; p 64 Andrew Redington; p 74 Marc Feldman; pp 76–77 Stan Badz; p 79 Harry How; p 88 Sam Greenwood; p 90, p 93 Andrew Redington; p 94 Ezra Shaw; pp 96–97 Leanna Rathkelly; p 104 Chris Condon; pp 108–109 Warren Little; p 111 Andrew Redington; p 113 Koji Aoki; p 115 David Cannon; pp 126–127 Thomas Northcut; p 129 Stuart Franklin; p 130 Richard Heathcote; p 137 Warren Little; p 140 Doug Pensinger; p 143 David Cannon; pp 146–147 David Cannon; p 151 Stan Badz; pp 160–161 Mike Powell; p 164 Stuart Franklin; p 170 Scott Halleran; p 172 Tim Sloan; pp 176–177 Marvin E. Newman; p 178, 180, 182 David Cannon; p 184 Hunter Martin; p 186 Jed Jacobsohn; p 188 David Cannon; p 189 Harry How; p 190, 192 David Cannon; p 193 Richard Heathcote; p 194 Chris Close; p 196 Ezra Shaw; pp 198–199 Todd Bigelow; p 207 Kevin C. Cox; p 208 Richard Heathcote; p 210 Chris Condon; pp 212–213 Timothy A. Clary/AFP.

All other photographs are by Hart McLeod Limited, Cambridge. The models for the teaching photographs were **Darren Wright** U18 English Open Amateur Champion and **Oliver Turnill** Darton Georgia College Cavaliers

The author gratefully acknowledges the help of a panel of experts in the preparation of this book:

Christian Fogden Swing and short game guru; **Hunter Kane (HeartMath)** Emotional, mental development; **Robert Cook (Golf Ballistix)** Club fitter; **David Hicks** Putter fitting and coaching guru; **Anthony Boyle** Fitness adviser; **Juliet Wilson** Nutritionist

Illustrations are by Mark Preston, The Bright Agency.

Editorial, layout and production by Hart McLeod, Cambridge

Quercus Publishing Plc
21 Bloomsbury Square
London
WC1A 2NS
First published in 2009

A catalogue record of this book is available from the British Library

ISBN 978 1 84724 646 2

10 9 8 7 6 5 4 3 2 1

Printed and bound in China

Introduction

This book has been written to suit you. You are an individual and will develop *your* own game—your physical shape, where you play, what you want to get from the game etc. This is what this book does, looks at you as a unique golfer.

PLAY BETTER GOLF helps you look at the fundamentals you have already learned and start to build on them. It is about developing your game, in every area, so you can begin to take shots off, play more confidently and, as a consequence, enjoy the great game of golf more.

Importantly the book values an integrated approach covering all parts of golf, from the swing to what clubs you play with, from your physical fitness to the way you prepare mentally for the big match. What PLAY BETTER GOLF aims to provide is a combination of core technical skills with emotional intelligence, focused development and enjoyment, all of which will influence the successful performance of you, the golfer. All such skills and qualities must be nurtured and honed before your true performance potential can be realized. In the pursuit of sporting excellence the book adopts an holistic approach, focusing not only on the fundamentals of golf but upon all aspects of sporting performance.

Of course you won't be able to take everything on board in one go. Indeed there may be aspects of the book with which you don't agree and which don't work for you. Golf is a thinking game, you are an individual and your golf game will be unique; you have to develop it in a manner that suits you.

Ideally you will be able to dip in and out of the book, taking small parts of the advice with you on to the course and practice ground. Slowly those that work will gradually make their way into your game, becoming second nature. From time to time you will want to come back and work on something afresh. All the best players in the world are continually learning—you should be no different.

If you are keen on the game and want to keep in improving then PLAY BETTER GOLF will not be the last book you buy. But it should be an important and valuable step in the right direction.

Colin Howe

Equipment

Equipment **126–127**
Buying new clubs   128–129
Bags and trolleys   130–131
Woods selection   132–133
Irons   134–135
Wedges   136–137
Putters   138–139
Putters... and balls   140–141
Other equipment   142–143
What to wear   144–145

Practice **146–147**
Mental drill   148–149
Putting   150–151
The short game   152–153
The swing   154–155
On the course   156–157
Plan your practice   158–159

Course management **160–161**
Think afresh...   162–163
Reactive targeting   164–165
Attack point   166–167
Handrailing   168–169
Aiming off   170–171
Distance awareness   172–173
Course review   174–175

**Great courses and how
to play them** **176–177**
Augusta National   178–179
Gleneagles   180–181
Les Bordes   182–183
Muirfield Village   184–185
Pebble Beach   186–187
Pine Valley   188–189
Royal Melbourne   190–191
Sun City   192–193
St. Andrews   194–195
Winged Foot   196–197

Know the rules... better **198–199**
On the tee   200–201
Lost and unplayable!   202–203
Can't play the ball?   204–205
Don't get penalized   206–207
Take extra care   208–209
On the green   210–211

Reference **212–213**
Glossary   214–217
Index   218–223
Acknowledgments   224

Contents

Introduction   8–9

Great players and what we can learn from them   10–11
Bobby Jones   12–13
Sam Snead   14–15
Ben Hogan   16–17
Babe Zaharias   18–19
Arnold Palmer   20–21
Gary Player   22–23
Jack Nicklaus   24–25
Nick Faldo   26–27
Annika Sörenstam   28–29
Tiger Woods   30–31

The mind game   32–33
... mind game?   34–35
Motivation   36–37
Idolization   38–39
Your approach   40–41
Off-course practice   42–43
Manage your game 1   44–45
Manage your game 2   46–47

Putting   48–49
Thinking about basics   50–51
The set-up   52–53
The stroke   54–55
Movement dynamics   56–57
Ball motion   58–59
The perfect putt   60–61

The short game   62–63
Use your imagination   64–65
The pitch shot   66–67
The chip shot   68–69
The bump and run   70–71
The lob shot   72–73
Executing your shots   74–75

The swing   76–77
Myth of the swing   78–79
The grip   80–81
Alignment   82–83
Stance and posture   84–85
Weight transfer   86–87
Swing plane   88–89
Impact   90–91
Shaping the shot   92–93
Feel, set-up, execution   94–95

Out of trouble   96–97
Out of the rough   98–99
Trees and obstacles   100–101
Shots off slopes   102–103
Poor conditions   104–105
Out of traps   106–107

Fit for Golf   108–109
Back to basics   110–111
Aerobic endurance   112–113
Muscular fitness   114–115
Nutrition   116–117
Training programs   118–119
Golf exercises 1   120–121
Golf exercises 2   122–123
Golf exercises 3   124–125

Foreword

Golf is a great game, but one that none of us will ever completely conquer or perfect. The tests and trials it throws our way are numerous and challenging, but the rewards are immense—the feeling of hitting a perfect drive or a sweetly timed 5 iron, exploding out of a bunker to two feet from the pin, or sinking a 40-foot putt are quite simply unique and joyful experiences.

Of course, there are many other factors that make golf so compelling. It is the *complete* game, involving everything we want from a sport. There is a unique blend of mental and physical skills, the need for explosive action and calm poise, an opportunity for fierce competition and gentle sociability. Golf has it all. Whether playing or watching, it draws us in and engages us in a way unlike any other sport.

Perhaps the real fascination of golf is the fact that it is a game at which we can all improve—the learning never stops. This means that every one of us, no matter what age, ability level, or ambition can improve our scores and, in so doing, derive even greater pleasure from the game. Of course, it's not always easy or straightforward. Some days we think we have mastered a particular shot or technique, only to discover that what works one day does not always work the next. Some rounds will be going absolutely fine until, three holes in row, we lose confidence, play bad shots and pay the price on the card.

So how can we improve? What will help us achieve our next goal AND keep a firm grip on what we have already mastered?

We all know there is no single magic cure. If golf is the *complete* game then we need a complete set of skills to help us reach the levels of excellence and consistency for which we strive. You may be better at putting than driving, at chipping than long iron play, but you can't ignore any part of your game. It's only by looking at a range of skills, techniques, and ideas, in a totally integrated way that you can learn and enjoy it more each time you play. Improvement comes with practice and the best way to do this is to start thinking and playing with new ideas in your head and new tools in your bag… a formidable combination that together will bring you a complete approach to the game.

I am a great believer in the importance of personal development in everything we do. The strength of Colin Howe's approach is that he has drawn upon the ideas and experience of a team of experts, from all areas of the game—so no matter how you are performing right now, PLAY BETTER GOLF will help you do *exactly* that.

Bernard Gallacher

Bernard Gallacher has 12 European Tour wins and finished in the top ten on the European Tour Order of Merit five times between 1972 and 1982. He played in the Ryder Cup eight times and was non-playing captain of the European Team in 1991, 1993 and 1995.

PLAY
BETTER
GOLF

Colin Howe